ANNULMENT

ANNULMENT:

Do you have a case?

by
Terence E. Tierney, J.C.L.

ALBA · HOUSE   NEW · YORK

SOCIETY OF ST. PAUL, 2187 VICTORY BLVD., STATEN ISLAND, NEW YORK 10314

Library of Congress Cataloging Publication Data

Tierney, Terence E.
Annulment.

1. Marriage — Annulment (Canon Law)   I. Title.
Law   262.9'33   78-6790
ISBN 0-8189-0372-4

Nihil Obstat:
James R. Hertel, J.C.D.
Censor Deputatus

Imprimatur:
†*Frank J. Rodimer, D.D.*
Bishop of Paterson
Feb. 1, 1978

Produced in the United States of
America by the Fathers and Brothers of the
Society of St. Paul, 2187 Victory Boulevard,
Staten Island, New York, 10314, as part of their
communications apostolate.

6 7 8 9 (Current Printing: first digit).

PREFACE

When I was pondering the idea for this book, I conceived it as a useful tool as well as an informational manuscript.

It struck me as odd that no one had previously attempted to place into the hands of the general public a book treating of marriage annulments. I understood why this had not been done — the church or ecclesiastical churchmen did not want to go on record or in any way be accused of supporting marital failure or encouraging marriage dissolutions. What vexed me was the fact that a marriage annulment is a legitimate right that should be accorded any person whom the law finds to be deserving. Furthermore, it seemed to me that what is needed today is an approach that rather than seeming to support marital breakup, did actually assist in ecclesiastical reconciliation. What was needed, I reasoned, was a useful book which would explain what annulment is, how a tribunal operates, where to go for assistance, what grounds exist for annulment.

As you can see, the book is informational, providing the reader with a glimpse into a heretofore little known area in church life. As a tool, the book affords both lay persons and clergy with a working guideline for the proper presentation of a case. The sad fact has been that most people in the church are not aware of the developments which have taken place in church law that allow many more cases for annulment to be processed. This even extends to clergymen who have been hard pressed to keep abreast with the vast changes which have taken place in every area of church life since the Vatican Council. Owing to this fact, many cases which deserve treatment never reach the church court (Tribunal). Thus, almost everyone is in need of some type of general information on how to proceed with a case for annulment.

An annulment is a church declaration which states that the "marriage" in question, because of some defect, was never actually a marriage as understood by church law. Therefore, the church decrees the persons free to marry. The purpose of this book is to spark readers into taking their cases to a tribunal and giving them and their parish priest some idea of what to expect from the church court. Simply because a case is introduced does not mean the marriage will be annulled. Each marriage case must be judged on its own merits and the necessary proofs must be exhibited. This book is not intended to spark false hopes, but the reality today is that most of the cases accepted by the tribunal for process obtain favorable resolution. Therefore, the only way anyone will know for certain the status of their marriage in church law is to present their case. Some do not win. But no one wins who does not apply.

It is my fondest hope that everyone reading this manuscript will be inspired to help themselves and others to straighten out their lives and at length find happiness and peace.

Feast of St. Raymond of Penyafort
7 January, 1978

Acknowledgements

"Tribunal or Pastoral Ministry" reprinted from *Pastoral Life* (October 1974) with permission of the editor of *Pastoral Life*, Canfield, Ohio 44406.

"Canon Law and Second Marriage" reprinted from *When Marriage Fails*, ch. 4, © James R Hertel. Used with permission of Paulist Press.

"Conjugal Covenant: A New Look at an Old Institution" reprinted from *Listening/Journal of Religion and Culture* with permission of the editor.

"Preparing Couples for Marriage" reprinted from *Homiletic and Pastoral Review*, Vol. LXV no. 4, (January 1975) pp. 24-30. Reprinted with permission of publisher.

CONTENTS

Do You Have A Case?

THE TRIBUNAL

I. INTRODUCTORY COMMENTS ON MARRIAGE ILLS

It is one of the great assets of personhood that people in difficult physical, mental or emotional situations tend to remain steadfast, to stick it out, to hang on, or in current jargon to keep on keeping on." In no situation is this virtue of steadfastness more in evidence than in the problematic marriage. It usually requires little effort to sense that something has gone awry in your marriage. Frequently, only a visceral feeling of trouble is the indicator. You search in vain for rational standards by which to judge the degree of illness affecting your conjugal life, but to no avail.

Most people would rather discount the trouble than deal effectively with the growing suspicion that something radically wrong with their marriage is lurking in the wings. A typical flight from reality ensues and, while reason suggests a problem to be addressed, the emotions strain for flimsy excuses not to stare down these burgeoning disasters. It is not uncommon that the uneasy spouse talks to him or herself and says, "Oh, Mary (John) you are really making a big deal over nothing. Things work out, just let sleeping dogs lie. Perhaps its my anyway. If I simply forget these feelings I'll be better off. I'm getting too emotional about it all."

Today, across the globe, this scene is all too frequently repeated. People sense trouble and unwilling to admit to a problem, they deny it. The process remarkably resembles the mental-emotional stages of the terminally ill, which have been

CHAPTER 1

THE TRIBUNAL

I. INTRODUCTORY COMMENTS ON MARRIAGE ILLS

It is one of the great assets of personhood that people in difficult physical, mental or emotional situations tend to remain steadfast, to stick it out, to hang on, or in current jargon "to keep on keeping on." In no situation is this virtue of steadfastness more in evidence than in the problemed marriage. It usually requires little effort to sense that something has gone awry in your marriage. Frequently, only a visceral feeling of trouble is the indicator. You search in vain for rational standards by which to judge the degree of illness affecting your conjugal life, but to no avail.

Most people would rather discount the trouble than deal effectively with the growing suspicion that something radically wrong with their marriage is lurking in the wings. A typical flight from reality ensues and, while reason suggests a problem to be addressed, the emotions strain for flimsy excuses not to stare down those burgeoning disasters. It is not uncommon that the uneasy spouse talks to him or herself and says, "Oh, Mary (John) you are really making a big deal over nothing. Things work out, just let sleeping dogs lie. Perhaps its me anyway. If I simply forget these feelings I'll be better off: I'm getting too emotional about it all."

Today, across the globe, this scene is all too frequently repeated. People sense trouble and unwilling to admit to a problem, they deny it. The process remarkably resembles the mental-emotional stages of the terminally ill, which have been powerfully identified and treated by Elizabeth Kubler-Ross in her book, *Death and Dying*.

Yet, in a curious way, it shouldn't surprise us that death of body and death of marriage exhibit amazing parallels. Just as a man or woman will refuse, oftentimes vociferously, to believe they are dying, many terminal marriages find the partner denying the possibility of real emotional disaster. But alas, as with those suffering the loss of precious life, the partners to conjugal misfortune acknowledge a hopeless situation and prepare, as do the dying, for the inevitable. What becomes uppermost in their minds is how and in what manner, can the break be cushioned so that pain can be diminished.

Some people are more fortunate than others. They are possessed of a greater capacity for insightful reflection. These folks recognize, at an early stage in conjugal life, that their marriage is meaningless and, in a word, terminal. Many others are less fortunate. They "stick it out" and "hang on" until all the beauty, life, patience and kindness are washed out of their hearts. The breakup is inevitable for some, and by the time it actually occurs the two parties to the marital misfortune are cynical and embittered people. The situation which was supposed to create joy and happiness — spawned anger and hatred. Truly, a sad and pityful situation to any rational and sensitive observer. The subsequent question confronting the parties to the breakup is who can help them adjust to the aftermath of the mental and emotional turmoil which always attends such an unfortunate experience.

Lest someone misunderstand these remarks, let it be noted that one does not desire to create the impression that marriage is a temporary commitment, easily entered without forethought and quickly dissolved at the first sign of marital trouble. Nothing could be further from the truth. The ability to see difficult days through to happy conclusion is admirable and an unsung virtue in today's tortured world.

An alarming number of married people discover themselves "on the rocks" simply because the individuals involved refuse to care enough to try to resolve their difficulties. This is indeed a most regrettable situation and should be deplored. It is not to the valid marriage which has broken up due to a thoughtless and careless relationship, nor to those divorced from true sacramental unions whose own selfishness and cruelty led to their demise that we address our remarks, but rather to those conjugal irregularities and eventual breakups which were unavoidably due to the terminal character of the very marital consent. These unions were doomed, so to speak, from the outset owing to the slipshody preparation and personal defects which prevented a valid sacramental union from arising.

The church stands alone on the mountatin top, declaring the true beauty of marriage as a sacrament of divine love. Our great church will never compromise on the indissoluble character of sacramental marriage, just as she refuses to cave into her cynical critics in the other crucial matters of belief. When all the voices of doom have long since been silenced, the church will remain still, the most articulate advocate of love and life as it finds expression in the marriage covenant. Make no mistake about it — the church is not in the business of running a divorce mill. Her tribunals are for justice, not deception. It was God's pastoral providence and care which led the church to develop a system of justice for those in intolerable conjugal difficulties.

When other societies were developing yet easier ways to terminate a marriage, the church was engaged, through her theological, scriptural, and canonical advisors, in the process of making the justice of God more available to deserving couples. To be sure, the tribunal system has suffered from many and, at times, grave abuses, from both right and left wing canonists and bishops, but after taking all this into account, let us ascertain that the system generally works justly and more and more good people are being helped to re-enter the full sacramental life of the church.

II. WHAT IS A TRIBUNAL?

You may ask, "I've heard so much of late about the good work accomplished by the church courts in their efforts to assist broken marriages. But what is a tribunal?

Firstly, a church tribunal is a legal forum, consisting of a detailed and exacting procedural law, directed by a group of judges (usually priests but this is changing to allow for any competent person to be admitted as a judge) who examine petitions for causes (mostly marriage causes today) hear a case just as a civil court would do (witnesses, evidence, briefs, etc.) and apply the appropriate canon law to the grievance at hand and render a decision.

In the case of marriage the decision will be either that the case was null and void and therefore both parties are now free to marry in the church, or have a second marriage re-validated. The panel of judges and the attendant staff follow procedural rules handed on from Rome and attempt to process a marriage case as quickly as time, manpower and facilities will allow. There is usually a fee for services attached, just as with a civil court, but this is generally minimal in relation to the divorce expense. The money is not kept by the priests or staff personally, but goes into the coffer to defray the expense of the annulment proceedings. The purpose of the *taxa* is to cover costs — not to make money.

Furthermore, no one has been, nor ever will be denied an annulment process, because of inability to pay for the costs of court. For those unable to afford the cost, the fee is waived.

III. APPROACHING THE PARISH PRIEST

However, before a case gets to the tribunal, the usual procedure is for the parties to visit their parish priest or some priest counselor or friend who will assist them in petitioning the tribunal for a hearing. From this point most of the investigation reverts over to the diocesan tribunal.

Before we take a searching look at the tribunal, particularly at how those reading this book must evaluate their marital misfortune or perhaps assist some friend or member of the family to seek tribunal litigation, let's address the initial step of approaching the parish priest.

Not a week goes by at most rectories without the doorbell or phone ringing at least once bringing forth a tale of sadness and disillusionment over a broken marriage. The priest listens patiently to the story of heartbreak and shattered promises. Emphatically he reaches into his heart for tender words of consolation, even while he struggles to offer sound rational advice. The empathy comes easy; the advice flows with difficulty.

Years ago, the party to a broken marriage, after spilling his guts to his or her priest, was met with these words: "I know how difficult it is for you but you simply must attempt to get back together. God wants you to persevere. There is nothing left to do, the church can't help you." Well meant words from a bygone age. Unfortunately, these words can still be heard uttered by some "modern, young" priests who fancy themselves enlightened. Oh, they are well meaning, but uninformed. Ignorance of the developments in church law is the single greatest pastoral disaster facing our church today.

Presently many priests no longer spiritualize the problems of broken marriages away, they respond all too frequently with the words, "I don't think you have a case." I've heard this phrase often repeated as I sit at my desk in the tribunal aghast and a bit angered. For this very case that stands before our tribunal, the one the parish priest said didn't exist, is in the process of being clearly proven to be a matter of nullity.

The awareness of priestly ignorance unsettles me, but I understand the problem: too much to do, in too little time, with too little help, too little resources, too little encouragement from others, etc. etc. I understand and appreciate the dilemma and so I choose to pen these lines so that you who need and can prosper from them might be well informed.

Don't misunderstand me, I'm not arguing for your avoiding the priests in your parish. By all means seek their advice and profit from their counsel and, let them assist you in petitioning for a tribunal hearing. The reason I bring up the topic of your parish priest at all is, so you who are met with those ill-considered words, "Sorry, I don't think you have a case," may be wise enough to call the tribunal.

The first rule to remember is under no circumstances accept "no case" for an answer. Push your plea until the priest gets an appointment for you at the tribunal or, supplies you with a preliminary questionaire employed by many tribunals. You have a right to a tribunal hearing. Justice demands it and the church's canon law provides for such cases. You may not have a case, it does happen, but at least your marital situation has been examined by those who are equipped to handle questions of annulment, who know the church's law and know when it can be applied. It is not up to the local priest to make the decision in your case — that decision devolves upon the competently trained tribunal — please use the means available to you.

It is lamentable that so many priests and deacons lack the requisite knowledge of canon law necessary to adequately perform their pastoral ministry. But the sad reality is that few of the older priests have been able to keep up with the accelerating changes in the church's law and, few of the young have been adequately trained in the law because of its downplay in seminary curricula since the close of Vatican II. The individual priests are not to blame for this situation (although every priest should make the necessary time available to keep up with the law), it has been an accident of history. So plead your case and ultimately, for the sake of justice, let the tribunal give you the long awaited answer to your question, "Can anything be done for me, Father, do I have a case?"

IV. HOW DOES A TRIBUNAL OPERATE?

The word tribunal at first glance evokes a cold, perhaps fearful, meaning and response. It sounds so formal and mechanical that one hardly considers it as a pastoral organ of the church. But the tribunal, apart from the coldness of its name, is actually a welcome friend for those caught in marital breakdown. It is not a place where marriage counseling takes place, it is a place where broken marriages and shattered lives are healed in accord with the church's law. It is a judicial forum in which grievances are considered and rights vindicated. Presently the marriage tribunal deals almost exclusively with marriage annulments. It is a court in which those who have "lost" in marriage might find relief from the stigma of living "outside" the church's law.

Firstly, the tribunal receives petitions for annulments from the baptized (even a validly baptized member of another christian community can ask to have his marriage annulled. As a matter of fact, the broken marriage of two protestants must be annulled before they are free to marry catholics in the church). These petitions follow a somewhat legal format determined by law and frequently take the form of detailed questionaires sent to a party, usually through the medium of the parish priest. Once filled out, the petition for annulment is forwarded to the tribunal and it judges on the basis of your petition whether or not a legitimate case for nullity exists, (so always be very detailed in your responses). In practice today the tribunal accepts over 90% of the petitions forwarded and usually proceeds to a decision. There are times, however, when no valid case for nullity can be ascertained from either your petition or from a preliminary interview. This happens rarely, but it does happen. So let's not kid ourselves. Yet, happily, statistics today indicate that if you are involved in a divorce/marriage situation, most of the time the tribunal may assist in rectifying your situation

The tribunal then proceeds to call you in for an interview and inform your former spouse of your request for church annulment, while requesting that he or she come in to tell their side of the case. The church is not interested in who is at fault — just in the search for truth, a search which hopefully for you will lead to a favorable decision. So have no fear if your former spouse decides to denounce you, or even blame you, or even if you are the guilty party, the church is interested only in the truth and so the above situations pose no liability for your case. Happily, today even when the defendant (the petitioner is called the plaintiff) refuses to cooperate, your case can proceed — usually with the requirement of further proofs. However, this is easier than it might sound.

After each side of the case has been heard and the testimony of witnesses heard and all the facts and proofs are in, then the judge decides on the basis of the evidence whether or not the marriage in question was null and void from the beginning. There is no need to go into the church laws and jurisprudence on what constitutes valid and invalid marriage — leave that complex issue for the judge to decide. It is enough for you to know that such a process exists and that the church is expanding the grounds for annulment through a developing jurisprudence. This picture is simple — the tribunal is a legal forum, manned by competent personnel trained in the church's law, and available to you if you are the unfortunate participant in a marital failure.

V. AN ESSAY

The Tribunal as Pastoral Ministry

It is certainly no secret that the general feeling among the grassroots clergy inclines toward a less than favorable view of diocesan chancellories. For good reason, the local parish clergy harbor a measure of hostility when dealing with a local curial official. Much of the misunderstanding that has arisen over the course of many decades can be traced to that proverbial "communication gap" and/or the built-in "question box" nature of the diocesan offices themselves. Seldom, if ever, does the average parish priest get to look behind the scenes or experience the good, essential, but at times tedious and ponderous work, which activates and typifies the chancery offices.

Unfortunately, not all the diocesan offices are afforded the same chance to exercise a recognizable pastoral ministry at the office level. However, this does not argue convincingly to the uselessness of such offices, nor does it render the dedicated staff less priestly in terms of their ministerial function. Since the church is a community, there exists many different and diverse tasks to be accomplished, and admittedly, some are more fulfilling than others. Nonetheless, each and every function of church life contributes to the building up of the body of Christ and assists, in its own unique way, the pilgrimage toward Sinai, about which the Second Vatican Council spoke so eloquently.

One of the more exacting, yet intensely pastoral agencies within a diocese is the Diocesan Tribunal (the word diocesan is used here, since a tribunal is not strictly a marriage tribunal).

Each day the staff of a diocesan tribunal is presented with cases treating of the broken lives and unrequited love that is the experience of many Christian marriages. While individual problems are dealt with in case form, nowhere is this viewed as merely an exercise in ecclesiastic jurisprudence. That marriage cases are the subject of the church's jurisprudence in no way narrows the handling of cases to pure jurisprudence, rather these good people represent to the tribunal judges, persons who have suffered and are now looking for reconciliation in one of many forms.

Backlogged Tribunals?

Rarely, has the Roman Church been in such an advantageous position to act in the manner of Jesus than when it exercises its healing ministry in marriage difficulties. One such avenue of reconciliation is the diocesan tribunal. We mention the word "rarely," since it has only been in the past few years that the tribunal has had the wherewithall, in law, to address so many cases in such a healing manner. This is due in large measure to the expanding limits of justiciable factors regarding grounds for possible marriage annulment. Moreover, Rome has seen fit to establish more expeditious procedures (e.g. *Causas Matrimonialis, Motu Proprio* of Paul VI and especially the granting and extending to the U.S. Church its American Procedural Norms until the new order of matrimonial court procedure is promulgated for the Latin Churches).

Yet, we have not moved far enough along the road which leads to justice. Moreover, the distance thus traveled in recent years, and the good already accomplished must not be overwhelmed by the horizon of all that needs doing. The time has come to acknowledge the church's progress and begin to make the present system function as efficiently as possible, while still striving for yet other momentous changes.

A large and vexing problem encountered by the local diocesan court is that the more competent it becomes the more cases come its way. The more people it assists, the more people one discovers in need of assistance. The more expeditious and judicious the court handles cases, the more the increasing number of cases challenges its efficiency. Sooner or later, in one way or another, competent tribunals become backlogged and eventually people suffer as a result. Indeed, this is a problem which can be lived with, providing the work of reconciliation continues to encourage the people of God to avail themselves of the ministry of mercy and justice accorded them at the level of grace-filled jurisprudence.

If one looks to history he discovers that the tribunal has viewed itself as exercising a degree of mercy through its canonical activity relative to marriage cases. Whether or not a marriage was valid and sacramental is judged by the tribunal to the extent that this can humanly be determined. The judgment thus rendered was seen as constituting a bestowal of justice and understanding tempered with mercy. To be sure, this was true enough as far as it went, but it fell radically short of the broader dimension which attends to the viewing of tribunals as pastoral ministry.

Today the church's perspective is more ecclesiological. The church views itself as essentially communitarian in nature and recognizes itself as a pilgrim community characterized by the presence of both grace and sin, divine love and human limitation. The inherent weakness of the human Christian community is everywhere acknowledged. It is quite evident from our own self-awareness that every Christian forms a microcosm of what the church itself struggles to perfect.

Healing Justice and Mercy

It is owing to this expanded self-understanding that the church has begun to imbue its formal procedures with genuine healing mercy and concrete human compassion. As the church acts in this manner via its ministers, it symbolizes what the Lord came to establish, namely, the ministry of reconciliation. As the author of Hebrews tells us, "the priest can react with compassion to those who sin since he too suffers from the limitation of weakness" (Heb 5:2).

Many of those seeking the tribunal's assistance have been the victims of cruelty and un-love. Others have been the victims of their own selfishness dragging down their spouses into the

depth of suffering. Be that as it may, the church ministers to all
and applies the healing grace of the Holy Spirit to both saint
and sinner, to wounded and wounder. The church, which
reflects the image of the Lord, is no respecter of persons.
Everyone must be offered the formal assistance of the Spirit.

It has been frequently noted that justice is the minimum
amount of love. That to offer a person justice is the barest
application of the healing charity which the Lord left us as an
everlasting remembrance of His presence. How far beyond
mere justice we are willing to travel will indicate our dedication
to the approximation of the gospel in the church's daily life.

The diocesan tribunal attempts, not only to establish
justice, but also to show mercy and witness to charity. At times
the hard words of Jesus will be needed as a gentle correction.
Other times might see the necessity for encouragement and
support as innocence is clearly in evidence. Moral certitude as
to the marriage nullity is possible, but at times this cannot be
legally ascertained. Oftentimes one knows that a marriage is
dead, one feels (sometimes very strongly) that there was never a
real union of life and love, but one has little evidence to support
an affirmative decision. The structure is fairly good but
inadequate, as the judge in an ecclesiastical court is always
dealing with intangibles and with a supra-reality which forever
remains inscrutable.

Reconciliation

Diocesan tribunals seek to offer a measure of reconciliation. It is to this purpose that the tribunal work is dedicated
and directed. The tribunal is pastoral ministry properly so
called, for it moves to bring failing human nature to an
essential wholeness. Exceptionally rare is the case which once
introduced into the church court ends up moot due to
reconciliation between parties. The reconciliation which is
usually effected is the renewal of faith and hope in the lives of

those seeking to be placed aright with their God and His church.

The need to be at peace constitutes the essential reason for the introduction of a marriage case. Since believers understand that the church reflects the mind of God in matters of faith, they approach the diocesan tribunal to be reconciled with the Lord of their lives by settling accounts with the church. This portrays an implicit ecclesial understanding of the church's mission.

The task of ministry to these good people is most taxing. It is difficult to listen daily to the tales of broken promises, misspent energy and shattered dreams. The tears and anxiety, so characteristic of many cases, only go to point out the fragility of human life and the need for Christian empathy. Many are the cases presented which require painful inquiry and precise responses. There is no easy way to be reconciled. The two-edge sword cuts deeply as it seeks to excise the cause of pain.

Our mission, however, has always been fruitful, even if not completely effective to the greater majority. One reason advanced for the successful healing of many marriage cases, lies with the cooperation always accorded the tribunal by those working at the parish level. Through the local priest a case is usually introduced, and after its successful completion, it is the local clergy who continue this ministry of reconciliation by drawing those involved to ever closer contact with Christ in the Eucharist. Expertise is requisite for successful and just results but it is the parish clergy to whom it has been given the application of healing grace, as their parishioners strive to remake a new life for themselves both at home with family and at home with God and His church.

CHAPTER 2

EXAMINING YOUR MARRIAGE

Examining your marriage for signs of invalidity is not as difficult as one might first imagine. So long as an accurate set of fundamental criteria is available anyone can engage himself in a searching evaluation of his or her first marriage. For the purpose of such an analogy we look to a recognized expert in the field of church law regarding marriage to supply us with the necessary informational guidelines to arrive at an enlightened and, hopefully, accurate judgment. Canadian Father Germain Lesage, O.M.I. has proposed fifteen examples of concrete elements which are essential to a community of conjugal life and to which the marriage partner has a right. The absence of any number of these essential matrimonial components to a vital degree would deprive the partner of an essential right of marriage and, in terms of canon law, call the validity of the union into question.

What we propose to do at this juncture is to take each one of the fifteen elements advanced by Father Lesage and attempt to enable those reading this book to apply them to their particular conjugal difficulties. Examining your marriage in terms of this criteria should help you form a probable judgment as to the possible signs of invalidity lurking within the marriage. After having followed this procedure, the next step will be to see perhaps in which recognized category of nullity your marital situation falls. The concluding stage of your examination will be to ascertain what proofs will be necessary in order to prove your case before a diocesan tribunal.

How did your broken marriage measure up to the elements necessary for a community of conjugal life?

I. OBLATORY LOVE, WHICH IS NOT SIMPLY EGOISTIC SATISFACTION, BUT WHICH PROVIDES FOR THE WELFARE AND HAPPINESS OF THE PARTNER.

The love which is spoken of here constitutes an interpersonal sharing of mind, heart and body, with a view to growth of personality. It is not a self-serving approach to life or to the marriage itself, but a higher communication of heart which always cares for and looks to the needs of the beloved. Through a conscious effort to supply for the other's needs and the promotion of mutual self fulfillment that brings happiness to both parties, a union of life and heart arise which is a sign of the grace nature of married life. This mutual blending of lives constitutes a sign of God's Kingdom and establishes the community of love and life that characterizes the sacrament of marriage.

Many people are possessed of a faulty understanding of what marital love is all about. The bond of marriage arises when in a moment of grace, two people give themselves to each other for life through an act of consent. Since one can hardly be expected to consent to a union which will be unfulfilling, a true marriage takes place only when the parties giving themselves over to each other actually are able to provide the love and sharing necessary for a blending of hearts. When the marriage consent, once exchanged, is selfless — that is each party places the partner's needs in a top priority, only then does the grace of the sacrament weld the couple together in a sacramental bond.

Marriage "In the Lord," a reality of which St. Paul speaks so eloquently, must be grounded on a lived faith. This mutual faith in God ought then to become the cornerstone to the marriage. It is the spiritual reality of grace and faith which is the foundation for a true sacramental marriage. If faith is lacking, love will be diminished and if love is diminished, the mutual blending of lives cannot be adequately realized. If this faith-love is not present, at the time of the marriage ceremony and is not supplied thereafter, one can reasonably assume that the sacramental foundation for true christian marriage is lacking.

Ask yourself these questions:

1. Was my marriage to _____ really a mutual blending of lives? Did we share our minds and hearts selflessly?
2. Was a deep faith in God a characteristic of our union?
3. Did we seek to adequately provide for each other's needs? Perhaps one of us was self-serving, thinking of himself or herself first and only secondarily attempting to be a loving partner.
4. How strongly did we communicate with each other and share in the grace of marital love which never seeks to be wholly self-centered?
5. Did we seek to provide mutual fulfillment in our marriage? Were either of us more concerned for our own self-fulfillment as a person to the diminishment of the other?
6. How strongly did we try to maximize one another's potential to grow? Perhaps one of us held the other back from true growth of personality simply because of jealousy.
7. Were either of us very jealous?
8. Since true love can only bring happiness, were we really happy together? Did we enjoy one another's talents, gifts and share our talents?

9. Read over in your bible Chapter 13 of St.Paul's first
    Corinthian Letter and see if your marriage possessed
    the quality of love spoken of so beautifully by Paul.
    Use Paul's definition of love contained in Chapter 13
    and see how you and your partner measured up to
    what Paul describes as the true nature of love.
    Examine each and every line and apply it to your
    lived experience of marriage. Then reflect upon it
    prayerfully and ask yourself, How did we measure
    up? Then ask yourself one final question — Did we,
    each of us, really exchange in our matrimonial
    (wedding) consent the same type of love described
    by St. Paul?

Having done this proceed to evaluate, as objectively as
possible. Remember, honesty cannot be compromised —
which of you was more at fault? (Perhaps both parties shared in
selfishness).

II. RESPECT FOR CONJUGAL MORALITY AND FOR THE PARTNER'S
CONSCIENCE IN SEXUAL RELATION.

As anyone involved in the matrimonial court will readily
admit, sexual difficulties in marriage take a large share in the
subject matter of many cases introduced for resolution. We are
not here referring solely to those cases involving sexual
abnormalities or aberrations, but also to marriage breakdown
which involves sexual difficulties of any sort whatsoever.
Sooner or later, in one way or another, sexual tension and
problems surface in most marital irregularities whether these
difficulties be a cause or an effect of the marital disaster.

The reason sexual relationships suffer in most marriages of
questionable validity (to be sure, the valid marriage endures a
measure of difficulty in this area, however, resolution usually is
forthcoming largely as a result of the sacramental love present

between the marriage partners) owes to the fact that sexual dimension of shared matrimonial love forms the highest degree of that sharing. Since sexual love is at the core of true conjugal love, any sexual tensions can indicate a deep seated problem. Lest one be tempted to misconstrue these remarks, let us assure you that in no way should you conclude that sexual problems always indicate invalidity of marriage. Clearly, this is not the case. However, it should be noted that many invalid marriages have a sexual problem as its cause. But more importantly, tumultuous sexual problems often point to a recognized ground for annulment or perhaps indicate the absence of a shared conjugal love. Needless to say, any examination of marriage with a view to establishing a case for invalidity must take a searching look into the sexual dimension of the marriage union in question.

In marriage, if a person truly loves the other he or she evidences an abiding respect for the partner's conscience in matters that are sexual. When this conjugal respect in the sexual area of married life is absent or defective, then one can reasonably presume that the matrimonial love itself is absent or defective.

What constitutes this lack of sexual respect? Firstly, in the area of birth control. It is not infrequent, especially today, that birth control is practiced as a means of avoiding the procreation of children completely. This would constitute certain invalidity. But, more often than not, contraception is employed as a means of regulating birth. This might sound like a naive, unenlightened truism, but quite simply, it is not uncommon that one of the partners experiences serious moral doubts about the idea of controlling birth. A particular married couple could find themselves torn over this rather significant and crucial marital component. Refusal to respect the conscience of the other concerning contraception can indicate a serious defect in their conjugal love. Perhaps this disrespect might reveal (given their deep division over so serious a matter) that the consent exchanged at the time of the wedding ceremony was faulty, and therefore invalid.

Oftentimes one party will force sexual intercourse upon the other, thus destroying the very meaning of sexual love.

Today oral sex is growing in popularity among married couples. What happens when one party finds this form of sexual expression degrading, "dirty," revolting and the other partner insists upon performing such acts? This type of scene can be indicative of disrespect for a person's conscience and morality. Forced violation of another's conscience is a most serious example of utter selfishness. In fact the entire area of marital sexuality is a clear barometer of the degree of selfishness within a conjugal union. The presence of selfishness to a profound degree renders a marriage invalid in the eyes of the church.

Test your marriage:

    a). To what degree was your sexual relationship fulfilling?
    b). If unfulfilling, why so?
    c). Was there gross selfishness involved in your sexual relationship?
    d). If so, on whose part?
    e). Did this selfishness surface in other areas of your married life?
    f). Did either of you force the other to engage in abnormal sexual acts?
    g). If contraception became an issue in your marriage, how big a problem was it and how did you both react?

III. RESPECT FOR THE HETEROSEXUAL PERSONALITY OR "SENSITIVITY" OF THE MARRIAGE PARTNER.

At first reading one would be inclined to conclude that this section treats of homosexuality in marriage. While we will discuss this rather complex marital configuration, the main thrust of our discussion will center on the respect one partner ought to have for the other based upon their sexual identity as male or female.

Homosexuality in marriage is not an uncommon phenomenon. Actually homosexuals frequently marry for a variety of reasons. Some desire to keep their sexual identity or, more properly, their sexual orientation hidden from family, friends and business associates. Still others have conflicting sexual drives which cause them to relate physically to members of both sexes. This is usually dubbed "bi-sexuality." However, the fact of homosexual activity places these persons within the homophile category of sexuality. Some homosexuals, but these are admittedly rare cases, come to recognize their homosexuality only upon entering marital relationships which demand heterosexual activity and sharing. Once confronted with the prospects of sharing physically with someone of the opposite sex, they are forced to take a searching look at themselves, and acknowledge their sexual confusion. Whatever the motivation for marrying, homosexuality can render a marriage null and void before the church (and perhaps even the state). If your marriage falls into this category consult your diocesan tribunal. You most probably have a case for annulment.

Let us concern ourselves for a moment with the broader understanding of "heterosexuality." Firstly, the word heterosexual refers to the unique difference between sexes. The meaning, for our purposes, applies to the respect a man should have for a woman as woman, and the like respect a woman should have for man as man. This respect translates into a sensitivity for the unique personal sexual difference between sexes. A man approaches marriage *et alia* in one way, with a particular male outlook and perspective. A woman, on the other hand, looks at marriage from a decidedly different perspective. In a truly loving conjugal relationship, both man and woman understand and respect the different mental and emotional approach to married life which attends to their sexual identity.

For example, a man will view certain marital problems in one way and a woman will look at the same difficulties in yet another manner. The woman will shoulder emotional pressures in a manner markedly distinct from the way a man might handle the same pressures. What personal touches the female personality requires for emotional happiness and marital integration will not be found in the male counterpart. His personality will require distinctly different personal touches. Thoughtfulness displayed in the form of cards, flowers and candlelight dinner, simple warm human touches, are treasured and needed by the female. However, the thoughtfulness which will warm the personality of the male (e.g. preparing his favorite dinner) is different.

The questions which must concern us here are:

a). How sensitive was your marriage partner to your needs and you to your spouse's needs?

b). Did your marriage display a lack of thoughtfulness to the point that the respect for the unique needs of the other led to gross insensitivity?

c). In short, were you treated by your spouse as a man or woman ought to be treated, simply because you were a man or a woman?

Examine your conjugal life together — if this dimension of sensitivity was grossly absent, perhaps even graver abuses redounding to the very bedrock of the marital bond itself were likewise in evidence. If so, then your marriage was indeed impoverished or perhaps could even be null and void before God's church. Since a lack of conjugal love represents a proven ground for nullity one indication that your marriage may possibly have lacked the loving quality necessary for validity is a gross personal and emotional insensitivity for the spouse's needs. Has this been your experience?

IV. RESPECTIVE RESPONSIBILITY OF BOTH HUSBAND AND WIFE IN ESTABLISHING CONJUGAL FRIENDSHIP.

You may have heard it said that husband and wife must not only be conjugally united but must also become friends. The concept of friendship in marriage is pregnant with meaning for it is at the very heart of what married life is all about. For a marital union in the true sense, you need more than a sacred ceremony and a state recognition. You need love and above all friendship. For if couples can't enjoy one another as two inseparable friends they cannot make it through the years of "loving turmoil." Only that "staying power" so characteristic of true friendship will allow spouses to live in a sacramental bonding.

Why friendship? Friendship is basically a higher form of love than the physical expression so characteristic of marriage. Physical in the sense of sexual but it should be also understood as a close living arrangement. In a word — marriage partners live in a fishbowl of physical proximity — materially — sexually. But the material and sexual cannot conceive love nor bring it to term. It is given to conjugal friendship to effect and build a loving union. Why? Because the quality of love constitutive of friendship transcends the material and sexual and rises to the heights of the spiritual — the grace-filled. If the bedrock of marriage is friendship then impotency or sterility will have no long term nor lasting effects. Personal, material hardships (money, job, etc.) will not shake a marriage to its foundation — the tremors of pain will recede, for something higher is at stake. Something more lasting and precious is at the origin of your life together.

I see nor feel no compelling need to enumerate for you the qualities of friendship. You are all too familiar with this from personal experiences. Rather suffice it to say that without those whom you love, apart from your family and spouse, namely, your friends, you could not long hope to carry on bravely in life's painful situations. Those same loving vibrations you experience between you and your friends must likewise be present between you and your spouse. If they are missing your life together is hollow, your love sterile and your marriage, quite possibly, sacramentally invalid.

Nothing as important or treasured as friendship can be built up easily. As with the inventor or artist who courageously expends all his energy to accomplish the making of a dream, so too the lover if he chooses to build a marriage which will last, invests his full energy in fashioning a loving friendship. There is no other way. Nothing short of this will do.

In examining your marriage you must focus for a time on the elements of marital friendship.

a). Did you both expend the energy required to build a loving relationship based on the Gospel love of the christian life?

b). That is, did you and your spouse work toward establishing and maintaining the necessary elements which make up marital friendship?

c). Was your marriage based on this higher form of love?

d). Could you honestly say that both of you worked to your limits to sustain love?

e). Did one of you work harder than the other at establishing friendship?

f). If so, which of you failed to give to the other true loving service?

If you must answer negatively to most of these questions, then perhaps the qualities to loving conjugal friendships were absent from your marriage. This being the case there is a better than even chance that the full meaning and reality attendant to matrimonial consent was lacking when you married. If so, you have yet another indication of possible nullity in the eyes of the church.

V. RESPECTIVE RESPONSIBILITY OF BOTH HUSBAND AND WIFE IN PROVIDING FOR THE MATERIAL WELFARE OF THE HOME: STABILITY IN WORK, BUDGETARY FORESIGHT, ETC.

How often tribunal officials hear uttered from the mouths of plaintiffs and defendants these words: "Father, he never worked a day in his life. All he did was jump from job to job. He'd stay a few months, or even weeks, and either quit or get himself fired. When he did work he spent most of the money on booze, the horses, you name it. It got so bad I had to go to work or the family would starve. For all he cared the house could have fallen in on us, and the grass used to get so high in summer that the yard resembled a jungle. He was so irresponsible that you'd think he was still fourteen years old."

Or: "Let me tell you, Father, the house was a pigpen, grimy, greasy, unkempt. When I arrived home from work she would be parked in front of the T.V. watching all those crazy soap operas or talk shows. And of course supper hadn't been started yet. She was so busy all day, don't you know. The kids were never dressed properly, and I often wondered if they ever ate properly either. Father, there is nothing more disgusting to a man than a dirty house and slovenly wife. Oh, and another thing, she would never save a penny — she never spent wisely, only like some drunken sailor — all nonsense spending. It was really awful, Father, just awful."

A sad picture of married life, indeed, but unhappily an all too frequent conjugal scene. Far too many persons marry while remaining unfit to establish and maintain a home. Unconcerned for the humdrum details of married life, the "bread and butter" realities of living together, these irresponsible folks carry on as if their needs alone mattered. Lacking a sense of domestic responsibility they create an unlivable marriage.

Admittedly not every husband or wife is possessed of a Wall Street business sense, but certainly a minimal degree of financial responsibility can be expected from sufficiently educated and rational beings. Mostly, the opening stories of this section are the result, not of imbecility, but of thoughtless, careless and selfish personalities. Since it can be assumed that rational persons would never consent to a marriage in which such irresponsibility abounds, it can be deduced that if a marriage turns out to be the kind about which we have spoken, then it probably is the result of a form of defective consent.

Be that as it may, the key feature here is that such slovenly, irresponsible union is indicative of more constitutive problems. These irresponsible marks of marriage are but a sign of deeper, more pervading difficulties which will surely surface upon examination. These problems can frequently redound to nullity.

- a). How did your marriage measure up to the demands of domestic responsibility?
- b). Was your marriage in any way similar to the sign of irresponsibility described in the opening remarks of this section?
- c). Did either you or your spouse exhibit signs of financial abuse?
- d). Were either of you unconcerned with the details of providing a decent home for the other and all that this implies and demands?

Take a searching look for yourselves — examine your marriage. See if perhaps your marital situation resembles the irresponsibility previously outlined. If your marriage approximates this type of irresponsibility seek the aid and advice of your tribunal. Upon canonical examination perhaps more substantive grounds will emerge (almost always this is the case) to provide for a genuine annulment possibility.

VI. MORAL AND PSYCHOLOGICAL RESPONSIBILITY IN THE GENERATION OF CHILDREN.

With all the recent discussion surrounding population explosion and responsible parenthood, it is little wonder that the question of begetting children causes some uneasiness. Furthermore, the contemporary social and financial crisis lends many to reconsider the issue of family size so as to bring the lived marital situation into line with the demands of practical living. Couple all this malaise with a breakthrough in the field of birth control and contraception and you have presented a most confusing set of options as regards responsible family planning.

It has always been counseled, wisely I might add, that extremes of any sort are to be avoided at all costs. If "virtue stands in the middle," (and this is not a plug for mediocrity) as the old saying goes, then perhaps regarding the generation of children, one must set his or her sights to a reasonable middle ground, so as to enable the couple to adequately handle God's precious gift of life.

This search for *your* middle course of action implies balance and stability; it likewise implies mutual marital cooperation and consensus. Responsibility is the key here. Married couples have a responsibility to raise a family, providing there are no physiological obstacles to this christian goal. This responsibility extends not only to physical procreation but includes the psychological responsibility of raising a family for which you are mentally and emotionally able to provide. It serves no purpose simply to beget offsprings. Animals instinctively do the same. What is typically human in procreation is the raising of a family in a suitable environment and providing the rational care necessary for human growth and development.

Not infrequently one stumbles upon couples who either refuse to have children or beget a family so large as to be unwieldy and out of the control of their parental resources, both financial and psychological. These are the extremes we alluded to before and these extremes are to be avoided.

It is irresponsible to engage in either of the two extremes. Both husband and wife must discuss their prospects for a family in an atmosphere of mutual love and sharing. If this planning is not accomplished (and I am speaking here in terms of the western world with its highly stylized culture and education), then one can reasonably expect marital trouble. Only through dialogue can the couple adequately assess their needs, goals and resources. Failure to analyze and plan together usually results in disaster.

Still another problem which is an offshoot of non-planning, is misunderstanding. Prior to marriage, many couples, in fact most couples, do not communicate their desires and goals relative to family life. Therefore, once married they frequently discover that they have differing points of view on what should constitute family life. This tendency to remain non-communicative prior to marriage carries over into the marriage itself. This constitutes an irresponsible preparation which leads to irresponsible marital living.

Procreating a family implies the psychological readiness to meet the demands a family will place upon a couple. It is for this reason that the church discourages hastily entered upon marriages, or marriage as an afterthought following upon extra marital pregnancy. This psychological readiness for marriage appears to be a necessary pre-requisite for the entering into a valid marriage in the eyes of the church. At least the current decision of many tribunals seems to be approaching many annulments from this perspective.

The preparedness for marriages includes the ability to carry through the demands of married life. One such example of "burdens and responsibilities" of married life is the generation and care for the children to be born of the union. This forms a large part of marital consent as understood by the church.

Proper sexual identification and sex roles figure prominently here. A father must become and execute the role of father. The same holds true for the mother. If a man refuses or is unable to carry out his role of father, both in relation to a daughter and a son, he is in a certain sense irresponsible. A child must not come to experience a mother being cast in a paternal — maternal role, nor a father acting as both mother and father. This is irresponsible and psychologically dangerous to the mental health of the children. Both parents must take an active and proper role in the education and growth of their children. Failure to assume their responsible roles in family life constitutes gross negligence, or indicates a psychological inability to be a parent at this time. Either of these situations constitutes a presumption of possible nullity.

Examine your marriage:

a). Was it in any way an irresponsible one based on the foregoing observations?

b). Did either of you show signs of irresponsible activity?

c). Did you assume your proper marital roles?

d). Did you communicate to one another regarding a family?

e). How conscientious were you both in the rearing of your children?

f). Did you beget children?

g). If not, why not?

h). Did you beget more children than you could adequately and properly care for?

i). If so, why so?

j). Did each of you plan for the education and growth of your children?

k). Were you both ready for marriage when you in fact married?

l). Did pre-marital pregnancy enter into the picture at all regarding your decision to marry?

If your overall reaction to the question of parental responsibility relative to your marriage is essentially negative, perhaps you have a case for annulment. Consult your tribunal.

VII. MATURITY OF PERSONAL CONDUCT THROUGHOUT
THE ORDINARY EVENTS OF DAILY LIFE.

It should come as no surprise to anyone that chronological age is no sure barometer of psychological age. Simply stated, age is no sure guide for maturity. Beacuse age gives us no certain clue as to the maturity of any given individual, it is eminently possible for a person to marry someone who is "old enough" but quite immature. This situation arises frequently in today's society with the result that many marriages never become responsible conjugal unions.

There are many number of classical signs which indicate an immature personality. No need to enumerate these signs for you. Furthermore it is extremely difficult to present a taxative listing of immaturity since immaturity can vary from individual to individual. Owing to this rather unwieldly situation, let us simply discuss some aspects of immaturity as they relate and touch upon marriage.

Maturity is essentially a species of responsibility. Anyone who claims maturity must prove he is responsible. The definition of responsibility includes the personal ability to act without superior authority, that is to act freely and competently without having to be told what to do. The contrast here to a child is obvious. A child is not responsible since he must rely on others to tell him what to do and when to do it.

Therefore, a marriage partner must be able to act in accord

with the above definition. He or she ought to evidence signs of free and competent activity regarding marriage and family life without having to be told what to do and when to do it. It presupposes the ability to conduct one's own affairs and those of others in a manner which equates with rational and intelligent activity. To be responsible is to be depended upon — to be reliable. Thus a spouse must be reliable — he or she must be able to be depended upon to provide a decent and loving home, to secure and maintain an adequate job and income, to have the long term vision to see possible option in family decision making and to provide for the proper upbringing of the children born of this union. If a man or woman cannot be depended upon to fulfill these marital roles they may truly be labeled immature. Dependability is a sure sign of maturity — its opposite is a clear and certain sign of immaturity.

Another aspect of maturity is accountability. The responsible mature personality is willing to stand up and answer for his actions and decisions. Therefore, a mature person will not be afraid to act, nor shirk his responsibility to answer for his movements, or activities. In marriage husband and wife are answerable to the needs and burdens of family life, and to that extent are responsible marriage partners. If one or other fails to provide for the needs of the beloved, then there is present a sign of immaturity.

In marriage, one must conduct himself in a manner becoming his or her state in life. The attendant responsibilities must be accepted and shouldered. No less will suffice. One may slip occasionally and fail to fulfill his responsibilities, but the overall picture of his lifestyle ought to symbolize underlying maturity.

Yet another gauge for judging maturity or immaturity is the presence of gentleness and kindness of character and manners in mutual relationships. The truly mature personality, although not perfect in attitude or manner, at least exhibits a degree of courtly graciousness when dealing with others, especially within the context of a loving conjugal union. Even in the presence of his enemies the mature personality, while perhaps given to a measure of anger and frustration, conducts himself in a basically decent manner. This person respects an individual's rights even when he would viscerally desire to "knock his block off." Such dignified demeanor is but one sign of a true integrated and mature personality.

Within the context of married life a mature and responsible individual is aware of the need for gentleness and kindly love. Whether it be on the part of the man or woman, this type of character trait is essential to marital growth. This tender approach to the spouse signifies the loving concern one spouse should have for the other. It is not only the decent way to treat others but the crucial factor in nourishing marital love.

To be sure, there will be times of bitter disappointment with one's spouse; to be sure, domestic battles will occur; to be sure, quirks of a personality will grate upon a marriage partner; to be sure, couples will become annoyed with each other over matters both large and small. This is human life and no one is perfect. Perfection is not the answer, love is. However, though little things will cause flareups, the benefit of maturity is that it keeps the flareups in their proper perspective. Maturity never allows small, insignificant difficulties to become marital disaster. Reason prevails, and maturity always shows signs of forgiveness and contrition. It is this mutual understanding spawned by a mature approach to love and life which keeps people together and growing. Treating one's spouse with kindness and understanding is a sure sign of maturity. Failure to be gentle, forgiving, understanding, etc. is a clear warning that immaturity is present in the marriage. How does your marriage measure up?

Still another aspect of marital maturity is "stability" of conduct and capability of adapting to circumstances. Maturity has always been characterized by personal stability, which allows for responsible handling of life's pressures, tensions and accelerating change. When one speaks of marital material, he or she refers to a responsible lifestyle which looks to insure the supposed permanence of marriage (of course, the church holds to indissolubility). This sense of personal responsibility for the care of the spouse will necessarily flow from a mature and sound approach.

Stability implies a measure of equilibrium. This notion of balance best defines maturity. Balance signifies a common sense approach to problems, a rational response versus an irrational or emotional one. In marriage, maturity can be identified by looking to the quality of the spouses' personal stability. Can he or she handle the demands of family life? The answer to this is quite important for a negative response could indicate possible grounds for nullity.

An immature personality tends to fluctuate widely. Predictable responses of such a person are hardly calculable. For this reason, marriage to such a person may be at best an unhappy experience. No one can be expected to consent to a union which will bring unhappiness and pain. No rational personality desires marriage to a grossly immature person. The reason is eminently clear; immaturity lacks stability which is a basic quality that will ultimately produce permanence. And permanence is what every love seeks. If at any given day you must guess at whether your spouse will be kind or hostile, gentle or rough, understanding or impossible etc., you have on your hands an immature spouse. Admittedly, anyone can have a "bad day" on occasion, but when "bad days" are frequent and unpredictable, then it becomes impossible to carry on a fulfilling meaningful marital relationship. Exasperation follows upon frustration, which usually leads to divorce.

Life has at the very foundation of its definition a measure of changefulness. It forever seeks growth; it craves evolution; it thrives upon movement. This quality of changeability causes many a person a sleepless night, but it also gives birth to love. The mature person understands this principle of growth — he learns to believe in the goodness of change — the beauty of creation. Beacuse he understands and appreciates stability, he adapts to those moments of change which creep into everyone's life sooner or later. He reacts to change not with fear, but with hope, the hope that this change in his life will ultimately bring peace.

It is given to no one to foresee when and where the forces of change will be unleashed upon your life. No one can predict the death of loved ones, the sudden onslaught of financial misfortune, the terror of a terminal illness. The way we handle our troubles will signify our degree of maturity. Since even the mature personality is brought to the brink of collapse when confronted with one of the above situations, it can be expected that the immature, when similarly confronted, will react quite irrationally. A good test of marital maturity is how the spouses react to the changing circumstances which enter into their mutual lives. It will serve no purpose to exposit the many species of immature reactions to life's demands for growth and change, for you are all quite aware of these. Let us just state that immaturity is most apparent to even the casual observer, let alone a marriage partner. The question which must be on your mind and lips at this point is, "Was my marriage a marriage of immaturity?" Gauge your response upon a careful analysis of the foregoing observations. Perhaps you have been involved in a grossly immature marriage. Perhaps, owing to immaturity, your marriage is capable of being annulled by the church.

Examine your marriage:

a). Were there signs of underlying immaturity present?

b). If so, what were they and how deeply did these signs affect your marriage?

c). Based upon accepted criteria for identifying the presence of a mature personality, was your marriage a union characterized by sound and responsible living?

d). Examine the approach taken to work, family, housekeeping, the children, neighbors, relatives and friends, vacation et alia. Can you say that your marriage showed signs of maturity and common sense in these areas?

e). If not, why not?

f). Did one or many areas indicate more prominently the lack of a mature approach to the responsibility and demands of conjugal life?

g). Could you or your spouse be depended upon?

h). Did your marriage express signs of gentleness, kindness and patience?

i). Did you or your spouse treat one another in a dignified manner?

j). Were signs of tenderness and understanding present?

k). Could you rely on each other for forgiveness and contrition?

l). Was your spouse a stable personality?

m). Did he or she show signs of a balance approval to life and love?

n). Was your spouse capable of and reasonably adjusting to the changing circumstances and pressures which entered upon your conjugal life together?

If you are forced to respond by indicating a lack of maturity in your marriage, perhaps you are involved in an invalid union. Perhaps too, upon examination at the hands of a competent tribunal, even more substantive proofs or grounds for invalidity might surface. This has been the experience of many involved in tribunal practice.

VIII. SELF CONTROL OR TEMPERANCE,
WHICH IS NECESSARY FOR ANY REASONABLE
AND "HUMAN" FOCUS OF CONDUCT.

IX. MASTERY OVER IRRATIONAL PASSION,
IMPULSES OR INSTINCTS WHICH WOULD
ENDANGER CONJUGAL LIFE AND HARMONY.

Self-indulgence and intemperance has long been a problem plaguing the human community. It did not begin with Henry VIII or Louis XIV, lack of self-mastery is evident among all of us. Perhaps we are in need of being reminded, occasionally, that the sins of others are basically our sins, that what we denounce as despicable in another is never truly absent from ourselves. A self-awareness of one's own weaknesses and limitations is a sure step in the long and, at times arduous, process of gaining control over human appetites.

Marriage has always suffered at the hands of self-indulgence. From the very origin of the institution we label marriage, conjugal difficulties have arisen because couples have lost the virtue of temperance. Even in our highly mobil and sophisticated society we have yet to conquer the culprit which has set couples at one another's throats — selfishness — intemperance — self-indulgence. Surely, we cannot cancel human error. Surely we cannot insulate life from its sinfulness, but surely we can be more discriminating when it comes to choosing a marital partner. This much is certain.

When we speak of intemperance or lack of self-control, we are not immediately referring to alcohol or sex, although, to be sure, these two are the prime abuses when it comes to intemperance and personal uncontrollability. However, these two marital "beasts" form but a single area of abuse. One wishes at times that such problems could be so easily limited to a couple of categories. Unfortunately, life is never quite that simple.

Take for instance, the compulsive shopper. (For our

purposes here we will use the female sex as our example, although clearly, this problem is not solely a female one). She reads the evening newspaper feverishly searching of new gimmicks or instant bargains. This is a daily ritual. What she reads tonight will become a financial disaster tomorrow. She cannot resist the urge to buy, buy, buy! Such limited vision is what retail fortunes are made of. Of course this wasn't quite so evident a problem decades ago, when cash was the basic medium of exchange. But with the advent of credit buying and revolving charges, the intemperate shopper has emerged. How many marriages have fallen on hard times simply due to excessive and foolhardy spending.

This example of intemperance is but one form of selfishness, or perhaps some manner of psychological over-compensation. Whatever the medical profession would label it, notwithstanding, the simple truth is that uncontrolled activity such as this leads to marital breakdown. Reason: because it bespeaks of an underlying thoughtlessness which pervades, sooner or later, the entire conjugal life. If you examine your marriage and the evidence of this type of approach to living is evident, perhaps there exists yet more serious reason for the failure of your marriage. I'd bet on it.

The classical example of intemperance is alcohol. This plague is more devastating to marriage than perhaps any other problem. We hear a great deal of talk these days relative to alcoholism and its effects upon family harmony and stability. Thank God we have finally recognized this problem for what it really is — a sickness. Hopefully the medical profession will be able to help all who are so affected.

But what of your marriage? Is alcohol a problem? Is it simply over-indulgence which leads to abuse and embarrass-ment, or is it alcoholism — the sickness? It is crucial for the purpose of annulment that the distinction between the sickness of alcoholism and heavy drinking a classic intemperance be drawn. Alcoholism is one thing — usually today, a substantive

ground for annulment, classic intemperance is quite another —
perhaps an indication of a more profound problem. (More
about alcoholism in a later section of this work).

We could go on listing examples of intemperance for pages.
You know these better than I. Suffice it that we are aware that
lack of personal mastery and gross intemperance leads to
marital troubles which inexcusably work toward the
breakdown of conjugal life. Perhaps, in a marriage so
characterized by these two culprits, a true christian union never
even existed.

The mastery over one's life has long been a "holy grail"
pursued doggedly by men and women throughout history. It
has always been considered a blessing when men and women
are able to be themselves and act and live responsibly. On the
other hand, it has forever been considered a curse to be one of
those persons, who cannot "get hold of themselves," who are
unable to "put it all together" or who fail to see the value of self-
denial. To be governed and ruled by one's passion is a cruel and
vicious way of living. Happiness is illusive and never attained.

    Examine your marriage:
        a). Was it a marriage based upon mutuality and
            sharing, or selfishness?
        b). Did your marriage possess signs of irrationality or
            intemperance?
        c). If so, in what area? (Frequently the area in question
            will directly affect the validity of the union).
        d). How was the problem handled?
        e). When did it begin?
        f). Who was at fault?
        g). Did you suspect anything of this sort prior to
            marrying?
        h). Were you ever warned by others of the problem but
            refused to listen?
        i). How did the intemperance, or lack of self-control, or

irrationality, or passion affect the reasonable functioning of your life together?

Ask yourself these and other questions. If you find that your marriage was an example of this classic problem, perhaps you may have a case for annulment. Let the tribunal take a look.

CONCLUSION

Today only the brash dreamers would venture a prediction that any particular marriage will endure a lifetime. The wise are never so fooled as to conjecture upon the future outcome of any situation involving emotional and rational creatures. The simple fact is that no one knows for certain just what elements hold one marriage together and which lead to destruction in another. However, many of the constitutive elements for a happy conjugal life have been spoken of in the preceding sections. The presence of selfless love, communication, patience and mutual responsibility are indigenous to what we label sacramental and valid marriage. The absence, therefore, to a vital degree of any of these recognized essentials can only lead to marital failure. Indeed, one can presume that a lack of one or other of the loving components needed for true marital bonding argues to the very invalidity of the conjugal union itself. Just because one goes through a wedding ceremony does not necessarily follow that a marriage union has taken place. Love requires more than a mere ceremony. Love requires a sharing of mind, heart and will. To contract marriage one needs to do much more than simply fulfill the legal requirements. Those that wish to share life together must be actually willing to share themselves. Yet even more than the desire to share love, those who seek to marry ought to be able, capable, and capacitated to do just that — to share life and love. The mere desire to share is not nearly sufficient; the parties to marriage must be personally capable of delivering on the promises made at the wedding ceremony. Love is such a misused word that it has lost its meaning, so that when many say "I love you," they really are not referring to actual love. Rather only the concept of love that they possess. Unfortunately, with growing regularity, what is said to be love is not love at all.

Let us now turn our attention to examining the heading or grounds for annulment with the Roman Catholic Church. Perhaps those reading and reflecting upon the expanded grounds for annulment might discover that they never really entered a valid marriage and that perhaps they are in a position to prove the same in the church court.

CHAPTER 3
FACTORS PERTAINING TO ANNULMENT

INTOXICATION AT TIME OF WEDDING CEREMONY

There are, of course, many levels of intoxication due to a person's alcoholic intake. The degree of drunkenness is determined by medical science on the percentage of alcohol within one's bloodstream. Since alcohol is generally absorbed into the blood at a rather fast pace, the number of drinks one ingests within a given time will determine the "quickness" of intoxication as well as the degree thereof.

Many factors enter into one becoming intoxicated. These factors vary from the amount of alcohol ingested. The true frame within which the drinks were consumed. The amount of food within one's stomach (since this radically affects the absorption rate of alcohol into the bloodstream, the more food in the stomach the slower the absorption, the slower the rate of intoxication). The type of alcohol consumed, the person's size and built, the person's physical and emotional condition, etc.

The blood will carry the ingested alcohol to the liver which burns up alcohol at a steady pace (somewhere around 1 ounce per hour). But when the level of alcohol exceeds this rate, the liver cannot but burn off an ounce at a time and the rest continues to flow in the bloodstream and eventually ends up in the brain. The result is intoxication in one of several degrees.

The discussion on alcoholic intoxication as a means of possible annulment is a tricky area of jurisprudence, and we, therefore, have chosen to prepare our legal observation with a short statement on the nature of alcoholic reaction in persons.

It happens, not infrequently, that one or other party to a marriage is intoxicated at the moment in the ceremony when consent is exchanged. Since in Canon Law, proper rational consent is absolutely crucial for the validity of a marriage, then it stands to reason that if one of the parties to a marriage was intoxicated at the ceremony, the marriage is invalid and can be annulled in a church court.

What type of intoxication are we speaking of here? What degree of drunkenness is required to invalidate a marriage? Strictly speaking, one must be "quite intoxicated." Just "feeling good" is not usually sufficient (not usually but perhaps this "feeling good" in a certain situation, etc. might constitute invalidity). Rather, a pretty well defined intoxication characterized by blurred vision, poor motor reflex (perhaps the person even needs assistance in walking), etc. This stage of intoxication might be indicated by unusual behavioral patterns, or a change in personality to some degree. If any of these factors were present at the time of your wedding, then I suggest that the tribunal be given a chance to examine your marriage for possible invalidity.

Furthermore, the reason and motivation for a person getting drunk stands as a key factor in the judging of invalidity. Perhaps the marriage partner was a frequent heavy drinker. If this were the case, perhaps the spouse was an alcoholic, in which case there would probably be a good case for annulment on the grounds of alcoholism (more on this later). Perhaps, the party to your marriage got drunk in order to "get it over with," or perhaps even to do what he or she really didn't intend — marriage. The why he or she became intoxicated on the wedding day at the time of the ceremony indicates a deeper problem or lack of true loving consent, in which case there would be no marriage present.

Moreover, it should be noted that today, especially, intoxication at the ceremony might be due to an excessive intake of narcotics or pills of varying degrees of potency.

Alcohol is not the only form of intoxication, drugs are yet another. The same rules apply to intoxication from drugs that apply to alcohol. But again, the why of taking drugs will perhaps be a critical factor in the determination of marital invalidity.

How do you go about proving that there existed intoxication at the time of the wedding ceremony? First, the best way is to call upon some relative or friends who might be willing to testify to the fact before a church court. This need not be done by a personal interview — a deposition from a witness is sufficient. Secondly, it always helps to have the allegedly intoxicated party "confess" to his being in such a state during the ceremony. However, this is not essential to the outcome of a case.

If your broken marriage took place under these circumstances, you should submit your case to your local tribunal and have them review its merits. Perhaps an annulment can be obtained upon this ground, or maybe upon investigation, yet further grounds for annulment will be uncovered. It is clearly to one's advantage to have the church's legal experts examine your marital problem.

Alcoholism

There has been much discussion of late concerning alcoholism and its effects. Medical science has conducted extensive testing in the area of alcohol and its effects upon bodily function, especially its slow destruction of brain cells. The social sciences have likewise engaged in the intensive study of alcoholism as it affects the social fiber of this country and the world, particularly the family unit. Sociologists now reckon that alcoholism destroys not only the individual so affected but also his or her entire family as a unit and, can have lasting effects upon certain individual members of the family, especially the children. Psychology then enters the picture to compute the effects of alcohol upon the individual behavioral pattern of the alcoholic, as well as the negative psychological effect upon certain other members of society who engage intimately with the alcoholic. Alcoholism has been classified as a disease by most professional men in the medical and behavioral sciences. The conclusion therefore is that alcoholism is more than mere rampant intemperance. It is an uncontrollable impulse to engage in a form of self-destruction (though perhaps the alcoholic is not trying to destroy himself). He does, however, usually manage to destroy his home and family.

Since alcoholism is a disease, and since it is impulsive behavior which appears to be present constitutionally in some people, then it therefore seems to constitute a radical impairment to the exchanging of proper matrimonial consent. The alcoholic, because he has no control over his "problem" probably has an incapacity for fulfilling the obligation promised in the marriage ceremony. Hence, alcoholism is a ground for annulment.

Father Lawrence Wren in his work entitled *Annulments*, states that the World Health Organization divides alcoholism into four groups:

Beginning — Without severe neurotic signs
Middle   — With neurotic characteristics
Chronic   — Without psychotic involvement
Irreversible — With permanent damage

He further states that "alcoholism does not affect the validity of marriage until it reaches the chronic stage." It is not, therefore, social drinkers or heavy drinkers or excessive drinkers or even all alcoholics who are under discussion, but only those in the chronic and irreversible stages. However, I would add a qualification at this point. While it is certainly true that annulment on the grounds of chronic or irreversible alcoholism requires that there be available clear evidence as to the presence of these two stages of alcoholism, I would add that heavy social or excessive drinking in any form may indicate a seriously irresponsible personality. Whence, there might be present grounds for a church annulment, not relative to alcoholism but rather due to some psychological or emotional irregularity. Therefore, when marital problems of various caliber arise amidst the context of drinking, a tribunal review of one's marriage is clearly in order.

Fr. Wren citing a decision of the Sacred Roman Rota (The Rota is the church's highest appeal court and handles marriage cases in final appeal from all over the world) by Sabattoni, dated 24 February 1961, records what Sabattoni posits as classic signs and characteristics of chronic alcoholism. Perhaps the following bit of description will help you judge the presence of alcoholism as grounds for annulity in your marriage.

Sabattoni's words as recorded by Wren: "chronic alcoholism is characterized by a complete decline of the intellect, of the memory and will, as a result of which the victim appears indifferent, unstable, incapable of concentrating attention or of persevering in a job; and by loss of the ethical sense causing a deviation of personality. The alcoholic gradually loses his self-respect, becomes careless about his person and about the approval of others, cynical, disaffectionate, cruel and obscene.

"Sexual weakness resulting from the abuse of alcohol not infrequently leads an individual to acts of perversion by which he attempts to satisfy his persistent libido. Under this complexity of psychic degeneration definite syndromes emerge among which are delirious forms of a persecution complex, especially quarrels or showdowns with his wife (or husband), rages of jealousy. . . These may be considered the observable characteristics or effects."

How does one judge the degree of seriousness attending to

alcoholism? When is one a chronic alcoholic? What barometer is applied to compute the data whereby chronic alcoholism can be determined or proven in court?

1) First, the church court will look for signs of behavioral irregularities and physical impairment. Some symptoms of chronic alcoholism would be occasional blockouts, problems in walking, motor control, the feeling of "pins and needles" in the extremities, involuntary tremors of face, hands, mouth, trouble speaking, etc.

2) Secondly, the church court will try to determine how long the disease has been present with the person. Of course there is no sure-fire yardstick to determine the exact duration of this illness, since the degree of the symptoms of alcoholism vary in time with individual nature and physical makeup. However, once the signs of chronic alcoholism are visible we presume that the problem has been a long-standing one.

3) Thirdly, medical records are always helpful to a tribunal's review of a case. These records supplement the verbal testimony of the parties and their witnesses and serve as expert testimony to present further proof regarding a case for nullity (here, regarding alcoholism). So look for the number of times a person suffering from alcoholism has been hospitalized for either physical or mental reasons.

How does one go about proving a case of annulment based upon alcoholism?

1). Testimony of parties (husband and wife).
2). Confession of alcoholism from the one suffering its effect. Since any person suffering from alcoholism almost never admits to the problem, if the alcoholic party confesses his problem it should be viewed as sincere and truthful.
3). Testimony of witnesses who could perhaps describe your marital situation and indicate what behavioral characteristics they themselves witnessed when in the presence of the alcoholic party.

4). Medical records: If the alcoholic spouse has been hospitalized for drinking or its effects, perhaps the medical records could be released to the tribunal. This is not always easily obtained.

5). Police records: Frequently, the alcoholic gets in trouble with the authority over his drinking. The violation of law can cover the gambit from drink and disorderly, to motor vehicle offenses, to acts of sexual deviation. The presence of a police record based on offenses relating to alcoholics can be a great help in leading to a legal presumption that chronic alcoholism was indeed present in your marriage.

A marriage can be presumed to be invalid and therefore annullable when the above criteria is in evidence or one or other of the above mentioned areas can be proved to a substantial degree. When one is an alcoholic, it is very difficult *not* to be able to prove it in a church court. Again, the reminder that because a man is a heavy drinker does not mean that he's an alcoholic. However, his drinking may indicate a psychological irregularity which should be checked out by a church court.

Remember, in order to prove that a marriage is null and void it must be evident that this was so from the time the marriage took place. If alcoholism or heavy drinking was present, to a vital degree in your marital failure, consult your tribunal. You may have a case.

A PASTORAL ESSAY

An Alcoholic Parent: It's the Children Who Suffer

One only has to look to court records, mental institutions, and deliquency centers to find readily available the prolific evidence that an alcoholic family produces damaging results for the offspring. Counselors in almost any field of pastoral psychology can attest first hand to the influence an alcoholic parent can exert upon an individual child's personality development. While the family situation spoken of will not produce an alcoholic child unless the child himself has an addictive tendency already existing within his personality, still the fact that this child can and often does become delinquent, in any and all areas, from school to morals, can be denied only at the expense of proving oneself at the very best naive.

The family is radically affected by the presence of alcoholism. Spiritually, physically, emotionally, socially and economically, the family suffers tremendously. The most disturbing and effective characteristics of this type of situation is that the warm love and tenderness so necessary for normal growth and development are painfully absent. Trust in himself and certainly in his self confidence receive death blows; then a child has no one but himself to rely upon for that much needed direction, care and affection. Oftentimes the child will seek the help necessary (this drive for growth and love is inherent in the human personality: the person always seeks this in some way) for personality perfection outside the context of his own family life and as can be attested by doctors, priests, and counselors, seldom accomplishes adequately (even with assistance) what is possible in the truly normal family structure. The search frequently leads one to "tie up" with the wrong crowd and learn from them all the wrong answers.

Just how debilitating this situation will be depends on a battery of variables: the person's psychological makeup, temperament, former education and influence, physical constitution, financial situation within the home, the relation and effect of other siblings and so forth. Although alcoholism, per se, is not inherited, the above factors coupled with how the problem was, or is, being handled by the parent in question will determine the child's degree of social, psychological, and spiritual adaptability. Is there a predisposition for alcoholism? Possibly, but conclusive proof is lacking at this time. It seems that the alcoholic atmosphere, of the home about which we have been speaking, does dispose the child to alcoholic tendencies if he remains within that situation, but whether it determines his future relationship to drink is dubious.

The natural psychological development of the child lends credence to the belief that environment shapes the individual and produces in this case undesirable effects. The total trust and confidence placed with the parent by the child at an early stage of growth is a key to healthy behavior. When, however, this confidence and trust is lost through the action of one or both parents, then the child experiences a feeling of guilt and fear: loss of self-esteem accompanies these feelings and consequently the child becomes threatened from within as well as from without, subsequently, producing insecurity which seems to be a symptom, if not a definite cause, of alcoholic behavior and personality.

Moral behavior is directly proportional to the values (of parents) appropriated to oneself during the formative years. The child as he grows, ultimately chooses for himself what kind of life-style he will follow and toward what type of goal his life-thrust will be orientated. Yet he internalizes to a certain extent the mores of his cultures, communicated to himself through his family situation and parental influence. The standards of right and wrong, good and evil which parents call their own inevitably become at least essentially the child's. The point being here that within the confines of an alcoholic family many and various attitudes of mind and codes of behavior become impressed upon the child as he incorporates his own life experiences with that of those around him, with whom he identifies. The alcoholic personality creates an unreal situation in regard to the possibility of normal growth patterns and consequently inhibits the child from ever experiencing the gentle, tender and warm love so necessary for true growth and the proper attitude toward good and evil that will allow him or her to see clearly what is right and to be done and wrong and to be avoided. The inherent law of human nature that man always seeks the good, that man's basic tendency is to do good and avoid evil can never be adequately grasped by the individual child who has always experienced a dubious morality. It is not that the child is determined or fated for spiritual (psychic) doom but that his vision of conduct is at best clouded, because his fundamental education and most influential teacher has failed to be a father or mother in the manner proper to true parental love, to the necessary parental obligations.

Frequently, as the child nears adolescence and desires to be with, and a part of, people other than his own immediate family, he finds the process of integrating himself into the social-psychological context of peer groups beyond his ability to control and adequately to handle. This process becomes extremely difficult. (It is difficult as such for the child of an ideal family situation and a normal homelife), and more difficult for the child of the alcoholic because of basic insecurity and fear ingrained in his life throughout the formative years. A certain amount of hate for the parent responsible for this problem emerges to create a basic hostility toward his family and his friends. The carry-over of maladjustment from one area into another is made very easy by the situation itself. This often results in confused roles which possibly can find their origin in the "status" which the child desires for himself because it has neither been acquired per se (in the normal sociological sense of the term) nor achieved (accomplished via his own effort).

His family members play their roles as they see them to be, but because of the drunk, the roles are aberrated and consequently are misinformative. Instead of having the different roles of each family member become supportive and well defined, they, because of the drunk, lack the directive and supportive elements required and are best loosely defined. All this creates a rigid and unproductive personality. The tension, sorrow, and conflict so characteristic of this home stifles growth and effects a sense of incompleteness and inferiority which could haunt the child for the rest of his days. The child himself becomes uncreative and unimaginative for his parent or parents are alcoholic and alcoholism by its very nature lacks creativity and imagination; it is a psychological and sociological rut.

The children of an alcoholic can be helped and guided by trained men, yet it takes a great deal more than mere expertise and interest to rehabilitate the child of alcoholism. The basic point of reference always remains the family unit and in order to properly assist and adequately overcome the problem situation, it becomes necessary to cure the family circumstances as a whole. For unless the tension and conflict, worry and anger, hatred and insecurity that so typify that particular family are rectified and eliminated, the hope for a viable and productive therapy is virtually nil. The parents themselves must be helped by the professional, and assuming that help is sought and cooperation is positive, the family unit itself can benefit and the individual person involved assisted in life readjustment.

It would seem that the separation of the child from such a poor atmosphere is a prerequisite for any attempt at therapy. Once done, then the parents themselves can be treated while at the same time giving the children the break necessary for proper disposition to therapy. A child away from alcoholism is a child that cannot be influenced by alcoholism. The move is, of course, temporary but absolutely necessary if the process of growth is to be achieved and ever to have any promise.

The unfortunate aspect of alcoholism is that the alcoholic usually will never admit to this problem much less seek treatment until he "hits bottom." Once he experiences his state as devoid of joy and promise then and only then will the average alcoholic seek help. Until such time, it is the children who suffer most severely from lack of love and the desire to be what they have been destined to become: normal, healthy sons of God.

IMPOTENCY

It is not altogether uncommon that sexual difficulties constitute a grave threat to the viable future of a marital union. It matters little whether the sexual difficulty originates with a physical defect or is traceable to psychological causes. What is important is that in marriage the sexual dimension constitutes an intrinsic component of conjugal life and, since it is the most profound means of sharing love, any obstruction or deviation in this delicate area redounds to the very core of the marital union. Whence, sexual problems are closely allied with invalidity. The crucial factor in an annulment proceeding is that the alleged sexual difficulty has proven to be a major block to the establishment of a loving and mutual relationship, and that this difficulty has been present (even potentially) throughout one's marriage from the beginning.

Let us begin at the outset to clarify a frequently mistaken notion. Impotence is not sterility and sterility does not constitute impotence. Many believe that the inability to pro-create due to the physical absence or debility of sperm or ova constitutes impotency. This is simply not true. The inability to pro-create is what is labeled *sterility*. At times sterility and impotency will co-exist in a person so that one is rendered incapable both of adequately performing the sexual act and incapable of pro-creating due to a defect in sperm or ova. However, only impotency invalidate a marriage. Sterility does not.

Impotency is a very complex medical and/or psychological defect. It does not lend itself to facile discussion or resolution. We are not equipped to go into the complicated medical terminology or explanation surrounding impotency. We will leave that phase of the discussion to competent medical authorities. What we are here concerned with is the fact of impotency as a ground for church annulment. We will try in this section to outline the problem of impotency, its presence in a person, and what is required to prove this in a church court.

A. *Impotency in the Male*

We are here referring to the inability of a man to have or sustain an erection of the penis and to ejaculate into a woman's vagina. This is the operative definition of male impotency. The composition of the ejaculate is not at issue here. What is at issue is the ability to perform the sexual act. Impotency is commonly held to be divided into two classes: (1) organic and (2) functional. Organic impotence is present when the actual sexual organ itself is deformed or in some way organically defective. Whereas in functional impotency the sexual organs remain physically and organically intact but for some reason do not function in a natural manner.

Examples of organic impotency would be: (1). Lack of a penis. (2). Irregular formation of penis so that it cannot be properly inserted into the vagina. a). Too large for the woman's vagina. b). The so-called "bent nail syndrome" whereby the penis is so crooked as to prevent its being inserted into the woman. c). No opening in head of penis, etc. (3). Any defect in the penis, testicle or the sperm ducts which would prevent the spermatozoa from being ejaculated. No sperm — impotency. (Here note that while this also constitutes sterility, it is not the only form of sterility. A very low sperm count can render one sterile insofar as he cannot impregnate a woman. But while an extremely low sperm count is sterility, it does not of itself constitute impotency).

Examples of functional impotency:

(1). The disfunction of sexual organs due to any form of lower body paralysis. An injury to the central nervous system which affects the sexual functioning of a man renders one impotent.

(2). Sexual disfunction due to a psychological cause. a). Pre-mature ejaculation. b). No ejaculation due to some emotional difficulty. c). Inability to have or sustain an erection long enough to perform the sexual act.

How can one prove impotency?

Owing to the complexity of this ground of nullity, much of the sifting through and evaluation of facts is left to the canonical judge. He will apply the law in a case and interpret the application of the law on the basis of his own knowledge, and the existing jurisprudence in the area under discussion. The categories of erection, penetration, ejaculation, and semen in the vagina etc. should not concern those reading this work. It is sufficient for our purposes that you recognize a problem in this area of your married life, that it has caused irreversible conjugal damage, and that you understand that only a church court can adequately analyze this situation of impotency.

To prove your case, generally you will need:

1). Your own testimony to the condition of impotence
2). Hopefully your impotent partner's statement of the condition. (Although obtaining his testimony can prove to be a difficulty since many persons are too embarrassed to admit they are, or were at time of marriage, impotent)
3). Witnesses who are relatives or friends with whom the impotent party spoke and to whom he related the presence of a sexual problem
4). Expert witnesses, namely, a doctor's report (if the husband was treated or spoke to a doctor) which could be either a medical doctor or a psychologist or psychiatrist — or, husband may be willing to submit to a medical or psychological examination for the

purpose of obtaining the annulment, which may also help him medically and/or psychologically.

If your husband has had this problem and your marriage has fallen apart consult your tribunal in the Chancery Office for assistance in the possible attaining of a church annulment.

B. *Impotency in the Female*

Since impotency in the female is relatively the same in cause as impotency in the male and essentially the same proofs for annulment are required, we will limit our present discussion to the fact of female impotency and its form.

Let us begin again citing Fr. Wren's work on *Annulments*, p. 13-14. He says, "Although physicians do not usually use the term 'impotence' in reference to women, they would understand this definition to refer to an inability to have intercourse or to consummate the marriage. That is, to an incapacity of the vagina to receive the male member. . . The human action for the *man* is depositing true seed in the vagina. The human action for the *woman* is receiving that seed in the vagina and transmitting it toward the uterus. If the man and woman can do this much they are potent. If they cannot, they are impotent. What happens afterwards does not, therefore, refer to the question of potency, but to the "question of fertility."

It is clearly evident that the inability to copulate renders one impotent. Fertility is not at issue here. If the woman cannot for some physical or psychological reason consummate the marriage, then she is understood to be impotent.

The forms of impotence in the female are more extensive than the categories of impotency affecting the male. Here are a few examples:

1). Lack of vagina. In this case the woman is usually born without a true, properly functioning vagina.
2). Some defect in the size or shape of the vagina

thereby rendering its incapability of properly
receiving the male organ, e.g. too narrow — small.

3). A hysterectomy renders a woman impotent. (To
qualify this statement it must be noted that for the
purposes of an annulment this must have taken
place prior to the marriage. Also, a hysterectomy
does not prevent intercourse, but does prevent the
possibility of semen reaching the uterus which is a
legal requirement for potency. The vagina is usually
closed at the interior end in this type of operation.
This generally means a *total hysterectomy*).

4). Absence of a canal or the occlusion of the canal so
that it terminates without leading to the uterus.

Examples of Functional Impotency in the Female

This mainly refers to the so-called disfunction *vaginismus*.
In Wren's book he posits the following definition for
vaginismus, p. 16: "Vaginismus may be defined as the painful
spasm of all the muscles surrounding and supporting the
vagina. . . Which happens when intercourse is attempted or
even when the area is merely touched and which renders
intercourse impossible."

Vaginismus can be caused by physical injury or some form
of organ (genital) structural defect in the vagina. Or it can
result from psychological causes which produce involuntary
muscle spasm in the vagina whenever the male approaches the
female to perform the sexual act. The causes for this psycho-
physiological reaction are numerous and only after examination can one be certain as to why the woman so reacts.

The requirements for proof of female impotency are
substantially the same as those for a male. Again, however, the
tribunal should be given the facts for examination since they
alone are in a position to render an adequate judgment, taking
all the various complexities of this type of case into account.

If your wife suffered from an organic or functional form of impotency, submit your case to the tribunal — there is a good chance that it can be annulled.

EPILEPSY

Certainly epilepsy is one of the least understood illnesses on medical record. For decades people who suffered from epileptic seizures were characterized as insane and frequently treated like animals. Fortunately, advances in the medical and psychological sciences have shed great light upon epilepsy as a disorder of the brain and nervous system. Nonetheless, this disorder remains highly complex and profoundly difficult to explain to any layman's satisfaction. Clearly, it takes a doctor to understand the complexities of epilepsy so we will discuss this topic only briefly, highlighting the main points voiced in annulment cases, based upon this disorder.

Epilepsy is characterized essentially by convulsive attacks originating in the central nervous system of the higher brain stem. Although there are various forms and stages of the disorder, a central element remains throughout which has particular import for tribunal personnel. The element of which I speak is the effect of epilepsy which dulls, vitiates, or otherwise impairs the mind and which may prevent a person from giving proper consent to a marriage.

In the extreme, epilepsy is a major brain disorder which leaves the afflicted with a psychotic mental state tantamount to insanity. However, the important factor for our discussion is that while an epileptic seizure usually lasts for a short interval, it can leave temporary effects which impair a person's mental and motor process for days.

Therefore, if a person who suffers from epilepsy undergoes a seizure immediately prior to their wedding ceremony (this could be from a few days before, to the wedding itself), their brain could be so effected as to prevent their exchanging proper matrimonial consent. Remember, if consent is not properly exchanged, the marriage is null and void on the grounds of defective consent.

If per chance in your marriage you or your partner suffer from epilepsy and sustained a seizure just prior to the wedding ceremony, you may have a good chance for obtaining a church annulment.

As an aside: there are situations of epilepsy whereby a person is rendered mentally ill by the disorder — this too would render a marriage null and void, but these cases would require much more detailed explanations, so we omit them here. It is enough that the concept of epilepsy as a ground for annulment in the church has been posited and the reader made aware of the possibility for resolution of his or her marriage difficulty in a church court, on this ground.

Once the tribunal has been approached and your case introduced, the priest will then discuss with you what will be needed to prove your case on the grounds of epilepsy.

THE PSYCHIC OR PSYCHOLOGICAL BASIS FOR ANNULMENT

With the advent of psychology in the last century, but particularly the tremendous advance in this science over the past few decades, we have come to understand to a profound degree, the intrinsic effects a mental or emotional disorder has upon one's entering and sustaining a valid marriage. The church, which has long accepted the conclusion of medical science, has not dragged its feet in admitting psychological disorder as grounds for church annulment. In fact, the frequency of annulments based upon psychic causes has grown so steadily in the past few years, that one is astounded at the high percentage of marriages which break up due to a psychological impairment. One wonders if perhaps many marriages are being entered into which have no business taking place. Even so, what comes across clearly to those involved in marriage work is that most marriages today which go "on the rocks" can trace their failure to some form of a psychological cause.

Many forms of psychological irregularities exist, all of which can ultimately lead to marital breakdown sooner or later. What characterizes these irregularities is a profound lack of maturity, discretion, freedom, rational thinking, etc. The psychological disorder does not have to be so grave as to constitute clinical illness — classic insanity. All that need be present is a disorder serious enough to render one either lacking the full capacity to posit proper and true matrimonial consent at the time of the wedding ceremony, or the inability to fulfill the obligation of marriage promised in the ceremony. It is one thing to say, "I want to marry you," it is quite another to be able to have an ordered married life with all the responsibility this entails. What poses for love before the wedding may not be love at all when it is asked to stand either the test of time or the pressure of responsible conjugal living. What we are saying is simply knowing what marriage is supposed to be and actually being able to live it with a single, chosen partner can be two entirely distinct situations. One might be in a sufficient mental state to desire a particular job but unable to actually perform the desired work — usually the person gets fired or quits. This is the way that it can be for some people when choosing marriage: they desire to marry but once wedded cannot live up to the demands of married life.

Any form of serious mental illness usually leads, upon investigation, to grounds for a church annulment. While not every person afflicted with a mental or emotional disorder is an appropriate subject for an annulment, nevertheless, today the greater majority of cases introduced into a church court find favorable resolution, after the tribunal judge thoroughly examines the merits of a particular case. Given valid psychological grounds for annulment, the overwhelming percentage of plaintiffs provide the necessary facts to prove

62 ANNULMENT

their case in a tribunal. Therefore, if your broken marriage was plagued by attitudes, actions and circumstances which would lead you to believe that some serious form of psychological impairment was present in your conjugal union, then it would serve you well to bring your case to a competent tribunal. The tribunal will then examine the merits of your case and raw percentage alone (with any promises) indicate that the odds are good your marriage can be annulled.

To cite but one example of a serious mental disorder which usually (not always) renders a marriage capable of annulment, let us take the case and characteristics of the sociopath. (This term is now inclusive of what was previously dubbed psychopath). The characteristics of a sociopath have been described by the psychiatric profession as follows in *The Diagnostic and Statistical Manual of the American Psychiatric Association*, p. 30:

Sociopathy refers to chronically antisocial individuals who are always in trouble, profiting neither from experience nor punishment, and maintaining no real loyalties to any person, group, or code. They are frequently callous and rude, showing marked emotional immaturity, with lack of sense of responsibility, lack of judgment, and an ability to rationalize their behavior so that it appears warranted, reasonable and justified.

Cleckly speaks of this also. "Considering a longitudinal section of his (sociopathic) life, his behavior gives such an impression of gratuitous, jolly and nonsensical activity in such massive accumulation that it is hard to avoid the conclusion that here is true madness — madness in a sense quite as vivid as that conveyed to the imaginative layman — by the terrible word 'lunatic.' With the further consideration that all this skein of apparent madness has been woven by a person of (technically) unimpaired and superior intellectual powers and universally regarded as sane, the fact is that we are confronted by a serious type of genuine disorder. Not merely a surmise but a strong conviction arises that this apparent sanity is a sanity in name only. When we consider his actual performance, evidence of mental competency is sorely lacking. We find instead a spectacle that suggests madness in excelsis" (Harvey Cleckly, *The Mask of Sanity,* p. 400).

Does the above mentioned description seem at all familiar to you? Perhaps some of the "qualities" of a sociopath spoken of by the medical profession were present in your marriage partner. If they were, you should submit your annulment case to a tribunal for examination. You may just have a serious case for annulment.

As with all cases of a psychological nature, there frequently is present indication for other yet more traditional grounds for church annulment. It is not uncommon for instance, to discover that a sociopath has not the ability to assume the burden of raising a family. Perhaps he even has denied the right to children, or even the right to fidelity in marriage. The decided absence of these two elemental components of a valid marriage can only serve to further prove a case of invalidity. What must be remembered is that many grounds for annulment dovetail with amazing frequency to create a solid case for church annulment of a marriage. Perhaps one element or ground alone will not be sufficient to prove your case, but once examined, a tribunal often discovers still more pervasive grounds for annulment. Unsurprisingly, while one ground alone will not suffice for the arguing of an annulment case, all the other indications for annulment which surface in a thorough marital investigation, taken together argue to its invalidity in church law.

BASIC OR GROSS IMMATURITY

When one speaks of immaturity, the usual thoughts conjured up are those of youthful abandon, whereby the immature are viewed as those of a young age. Clearly, age is not the issue here. Rather, the issue is the mental and emotional

ability to meet the demands of responsible living in a way that
indicates an overall personal stability. Immaturity refers more
to the personality than the age of an individual (although the
two frequently coincide).

Some of the characteristics of a grossly immature
personality are:

1). Poor judgment in fundamentally important matters
   affecting one's life and his contact with others.
2). Egotistical behavior: A self-seeking, jealous, and
   immoral approach to life and other people with
   whom the person associates.
3). Emotional instability of varying degrees.
4). Signs of hostility, disgust of others, and fear that
   people are against him; a suspiciousness of people in
   general. In a word an antisocial approach to life
   (antisocial in terms of being against (anti) people
   (social).
5). Seeks self-gratification. As a child the immature
   person thinks of himself first and usually only of
   himself and what will make *him* happy.

The immature personality usually ends up with a broken
marriage, and yes, even a string of broken marriages. The
grossly immature tend to repeat their mistakes — they do not
learn from past failures or situations. These persons are
flippant enough when single but the worst indication of
immaturity only surfaces once they plunge into the burden and
responsibilities of married life. They are ill-equipped to handle
an intense interpersonal relationship of any kind, but most
especially the quality of love and sharing demanded of a
spouse.

It is quite obvious to anyone what we mean here by gross
immaturity. At times it will be a form of psychological
disorder, but frequently it is not that scientifically verifiable.
The signs of immaturity are clear to any rational, mature

observer. To have had the elements of basic immaturity present in a marriage is to have probable grounds for a tribunal case. If you have been the unhappy party to a marriage in which your spouse was a grossly immature person, then I would suggest you consult your tribunal for a possible annulment process.

To prove your case will be needed at least your testimony and hopefully that of your former spouse (although this is frequently difficult when immaturity is involved for the immature are seldom responsible enough to take a church process seriously). You should also provide witnesses who would be in a position to describe first hand your marital situation and the signs of immaturity that were present therein. Finally, it would be extremely helpful if a tribunal psychologist could interview you and your former spouse (if he or she will cooperate). However, the quality of evidence needed in your case will be determined by the examining tribunal, so it is best just to submit your case and concentrate fully with the investigation process.

By way of a footnote, it should be noted that ignorance of what marriage is or entails can lead to an invalid marriage. We mention this here because the two, ignorance and maturity, frequently coincide and, therefore, should be understood together. Although ignorance is a ground for annulment, it has been a long standing one. Today it dovetails with many of the psychological grounds with the result that most cases previously addressed constituting ignorance, are now processed under some form of psychological grounds.

HOMOSEXUALITY

We hear a great deal of discussion these days regarding the homosexual and his relationship to society. Long a sexual attraction whose very mention conjured up revolting and disgusting thoughts and elicited quick denunciation, homosexuality is now being treated and dealt with openly, without scorn. To be sure, this is a welcome development in societal reasoning, for the homosexual has a right to be treated as a human being, even as science seeks to help these individuals adjust to their sexual preference and looks to a possible cure for their haunting problem.

The Gay Liberation Movement has made a lasting contribution to society if only to have been able to bring this "hidden problem" of the homophile (generic name for homosexuality — from the Greek homo — same, philo — love) to the surface and thus insure its being treated as a problem. (Note that the Gay Movement does not necessarily view homosexuality as a problem). What has resulted from this openness has been a more enlightened understanding of what constitutes a homosexual and a more precise definition of the species of homophile.

While most avowed homosexuals seek out "marriage" with someone of the same sex, it is not infrequent that many homosexuals marry persons of the opposite sex. Thus we have a distinction made between the avowed homosexual (one who accepts his sexual orientation) and the so-called "closet" homosexual who does not admit to homosexuality. It is the "closet" homosexual who usually ends up marrying and whose case frequently winds up in a church court for annulment. Why these individuals marry is an open question. Perhaps they reason that marriage will "cover up" their problem. These persons oftentimes are not true homosexuals (properly so called) but rather are more bisexual than homosexual. By bisexual is meant one who is sexually attracted to members of both sexes. Consequently the bisexual can carry on a sexual relationship with one of the opposite sex (say for instance, in marriage) and at the same time engage in a sexual relationship with one of the same sex. At times homosexuals will (can) only relate sexually to a member of the same sex. The true homosexual is frequently repulsed by any thought of relating to woman or man sexually (much the same revulsion a heterosexual experiences at the thought of sexually relating to someone of the same sex).

It should be pointed out that under certain, unusually extreme or specific situations both men and women who are heterosexual have been known to engage in sexual relationships with persons of the same sex. Some instances of these situations would be: prisons, institutions, military service, camps, or any living situation where contact with the opposite sex is extremely limited for any number of reasons. These persons are not genuine homosexuals but rather engage in homosexual activity as a means of releasing sexual tension from unique circumstances or pressure situations.

In Fr. Wren's book on annulments, he cites Donald Webster Cory's work, *The Homosexual In America*, in which Webster posits twelve reasons why a homosexual marries:

1). Desire for children
2). Need for permanent family relationship
3). Inability to create permanent relationship with companion or lover
4). Fear of loneliness of older years
5). Desire or hope to escape from homosexual life
6). Deep affection for someone
7). Latency or repression of homosexuality
8). Hope of finding companionship in marriage; disappointment at inability to find it outside of marriage
9). Desire to create facade of married life, and hope to find protection against gossip and the concomitant evils
10). Aspiration for economic and social gain
11). Desire to please family
12). Inability or unwillingness to take strong stand in order to put an end to drift toward marriage.

These twelve reasons are recorded so that the reader might

more clearly understand not only that homosexuals marry, but why they do so.

Regarding the possible annulment of a marriage entered into by a homosexual, it should be noted that while the homosexuality itself is a recognized ground for annulment, it is quite probable that the homosexual's motivation for marriage was so defective that he also incurred other grounds for annulment which dovetail the homosexual grounds. This situation will be identified by the tribunal investigating the nullity of a marriage on grounds of homosexuality and the church court might then decide to process the case on one or more of the traditional grounds which will have become evident through the course of its analysis of the marriage in question.

People (perhaps you are one of them) who find themselves enmeshed within a marriage of this sort should submit their case to a tribunal. The chances are very good the church will grant you an annulment. The evidence needed to prove your case will vary, depending on circumstances and the cooperation of the parties involved. It is best to leave the question of necessary proofs to the tribunal handling your case, rather than for the author to suggest to you the evidence necessary and thereby mislead you. Your case may not fit the general pattern and, therefore, require more or less proof as the case may be.

SIMULATING THE SACRAMENT OF MATRIMONY

This means quite simply that one enters marriage not with the intention of entering a lifelong loving conjugal union, but only to fulfill some obligation or to gain something extrinsic to marriage (this is an oversimplification for simulation is a most complex ground for annulment, but for our rather limited purposes it will suffice just to outline the basic meaning of simulation).

For instance, Mr. X marries Ms. Y. in order to give a name to the child she conceived out of wedlock. Mr. X has no intention of remaining in a marital state with Ms. Y after the ceremony. He is only doing what he perceives to be the "right thing to do." This is a case of simulation of the sacrament of marriage. The marriage is invalid.

Another example might be Ms. Y marries Mr. X in order to get his money. Mr. X is wealthy or stands to inherit wealth soon so Ms. Y marries Mr. X so as to "get in on the deal." She has no intention of living her life married to Mr. X. Her only motivation is money. She has simulated the sacrament. The marriage is invalid.

Still another case would be marriage to escape military service. This does not happen now but, in the past when the draft was still on, men oftentimes got married to avoid being drafted into the military. If this were the sole reason for marrying, this constitutes simulation and the marriage would be invalid.

If you suspect for any reason that your marriage was entered into for some reason other than true love — consult your tribunal and have them review your case. Perhaps your marriage is capable of being annulled by the church.

FORCE AND FEAR

The two grounds must be taken together. A marriage is "forced" upon a person by someone in a position to apply force (parent, superior, etc.) and the pressures or force must lead to grave fear on the part of the one being forced to marry. This fear means that the party being forced is so fearful of the possible consequence of non-compliance that he or she submits to the pressures and marries.

A ground of force and fear is extremely difficult to prove in a church court. Owing to the complex nature of this ground for annulment, today we seldom have cases processed under this heading for nullity. However, force and fear is widespread enough to demand mention in a book such as this and, therefore, ought to at least be properly understood.

The most frequent example of force and fear is the situation involving a pre-marital pregnancy. This situation itself, should not be nearly as common today as in the past, due to the availability of birth control devices and the early level of sexual awareness. In any event, it is not altogether uncommon that once pregnant a girl will either find strong pressures being applied on her to marry or else (the else is what usually produces fear)! The boy might find himself in a similar situation when pressures to marry the girl he "got in trouble" become so intense that he fears the possible consequences. This is a classic case of the force and fear ground and while it cannot always be proven that, in a particular pre-marital pregnancy situation force and fear were present to a sufficient degree to render a marriage invalid, it happens that the case presented can be tried on some other grounds which can be more easily proven.

One best bet is to submit his or her case to their tribunal and have the tribunal determine if a case exists and can be proven from the existing facts and evidences available. If you have been involved in a similar situation perhaps your marriage can be annulled. It is certainly worth the effort to find out if you are deserving of an annulment.

CONDITIONAL MARRIAGE

It happens that in a goodly number of marriages, parties to the union place certain conditions upon the outcome of the marriage. These are generally placed prior to the ceremony and hinge upon some future situation or circumstance which radically affects the validity of the marriage. The placing of conditions upon a marriage is more widespread a practice today than one would suspect. What with the cultural climate encouraging the pursuit of happiness and fulfillment, it is little wonder that many persons attach conditions upon their entering a life long union with another person, which union could be the bearer of unhappiness. In countries outside the United States conditional marriages have long been a problem plaguing the church. These marriages were usually contracted in order to secure inheritance, or royal lineage, land, or perhaps political domination, not to mention the run of the mill conditions which are of a more universal character.

Now that everyone is sufficiently confused, let us give some examples of what the church means by conditional marriage or marriage contracted with conditions placed upon it:

1). "I will or intend to marry John, *providing* he does not drink heavily."
2). "I will or intend to marry Mary, *only* if she is a faithful member of the catholic church."
3). "I intend to marry Tom *provided* he has never taken nor will take drugs."
4). "I intend to marry Ann, *provided* she has never procured an abortion."
5). "I intend to marry *only* if my partner is heterosexual, fertile, or wealthy, or genetically sound, etc."

These and any number of other types of conditions placed upon a marriage render the contracting of marriage invalid. As with reference to all annulment grounds, the form in which a condition is placed, the intention invoked and the requirement for proving a condition, is a highly complicated area of study and we only touch the surface here. What is singularly important to remember is that there is a ground for annulment based upon a condition placed upon it by one of the parties to the marriage. Therefore, if your marriage is one involving a breakup perhaps based upon non-fulfillment of a condition, then the tribunal can be of service to you and will help you attempt to cull the evidence necessary for proving your case.

ERROR IN PERSONA

Briefly this means that the person you married concealed from you some grave situation or personality problem which affects his or her very person. The result is that you married someone you really didn't know and actually thought to be so different a person from what you perceived him or her to be, that in reality you married a different person.

People have an astounding capacity for deception. This holds true particularly when one is attempting to impress a future spouse. Whence they often conceal some grave personality defect which is covered up until the marriage takes place. After marriage, the reality sets in — "This is not the person I intended to marry."

If this situation has a familiar ring to it, if it is your marital ill then consult your tribunal and the personnel will assist you proving your case. As usual, the veracity of your testimony and perhaps some witnesses will be sufficient to prove your case. In any event the church court will do all it can to enable your getting a mented annulment on the ground of error or perhaps some other element of defective consent.

DEFECTIVE INTENTION AGAINST FIDELITY

We have already spoken about the concept of placing a condition upon marriage. A further expansion of this notion includes the "Big Three" grounds for annulment. These are an intention against fidelity, an intention against a permanent union and an intention against having children. These three venerable grounds for annulment have as their basis, some form of conditional or defective consent. That is, when one marries he or she places an intention to exclude one of the essential components necessary for true conjugal life. What happens, simply, is that the person about to enter marriage conditions his consent or renders it otherwise defective by intending not to deliver on one or other of the marital promises. When this is done the marriage is invalid.

In the case of intention against fidelity, the party entering marriage excludes the right of the spouse to a sexually conjugal relationship. The right to fidelity is a fundamental one. If for example, a man marries with the intention of continuing a sexual relationship with another woman and makes this an extension of the contract of marriage, the marriage is null. He has not intended to give his wife the right to fidelity. Lest the reader be mislead, we are not speaking of an extra-marital relationship which develops after several years into the marriage, say as a part of the "middle age syndrome." This might indicate the possibility of another grounds for annulment, given the overall context of the marriage relationship to date, and it would not suffice to render a marriage null and void on the grounds of a defective intention against fidelity. In this case, as with all marital breakdowns, the tribunal should be consulted.

The quality of proofs needed to support this ground for annulment is highly complex and to cite all the possible forms of evidence would serve only to confuse the reader. As with all petitions for annulment, the quality and quantity of evidence required to prove your case will be determined by the church tribunal. It is best left to the individual tribunal judges rather than to attempt a detailed discussion of proof which could only be at best general in scope, and fail to take into account peculiar cases with unique circumstances.

DEFECTIVE INTENTION AGAINST HAVING CHILDREN

The church has always held the view that children are

intrinsic' to the meaning and purpose of marriage and that marriage must be open to procreation and generation of offsprings — this does not affect those persons who because of a quirk of nature, or perhaps some other physical cause (accident) are not able to procreate. The church is rather referring to those cases in which the right to have children is denied by an act of the will: "I do not wish to have children or I will not have a child, or I never intended to raise or beget a family."

It frequently happens today that a couple will marry and decide beforehand to put off having children until they are settled, which usually translates into being, more or less, financially secure. This means that they generally enter marriage with the express intention of practicing birth control until such time as they are ready or prepared to start raising a family. This is all well and good and essentially a matter of conscience, but the familiar sequence of events generally follow an identifiable pattern: everything starts out just fine and moves along with both parties working to secure their "fortune" or insure minimum financial difficulties. After some time — generally a couple of years — one of the parties to the marriage starts thinking about raising a family. So the one party asks the other party for a child. The other party does not agree. He or she would like to wait still longer, perhaps a few more years. The spouse reluctantly agrees to wait but not three or more years. Time passes and the request is made again. Once more the same answer — no. By this time the marriage is getting quite shaky and before long it ends in divorce with the aggrieved spouse claiming he (or she) would not have children. What has happened is simple — the putting off of children for an agreed upon time was part of the marriage contract. When the one party requested the fulfilling of the agreement it was denied and, therefore, the right had been denied, since it is obvious the aggrieved spouse married with a view to raising a family. If he or she had known that this would not be, the marriage would never have taken place.

We could cite dozens of examples of defective intentions against children, all variations on the same theme. But what is of crucial importance here is the knowledge that the absence of children in a marriage has led to the eventual breakup of a conjugal union. Then the tribunal should be consulted. Even if an annulment cannot be obtained on the grounds of defective intention, it is solidly probable that the willful absence of children could indicate yet another probable grounds for resolution of a problem by a church court.

By way of footnote: once again the complexity of the type of annulment case makes the listing here of the categories of evidence needed in order to prove a case, unrealistic and superfluous. The best approach is to take your case to the local diocesan tribunal, where they will indicate to you what proofs are required by law.

DEFECTIVE INTENTION AGAINST PERPETUITY PERMANENCE

Living in a society characterized by a pervading sense of impermanence, it is reasonable to assume that "marriage for life" will be duly affected by this social attitude. Marriage is always one of the casualties listed when impermanence and frivolity rampage society. It is not unreasonable to presume that today a "divorce mentality" is foraging across America. This situation carries with it numerous liabilities for everyone and makes the entering into marriage a somewhat precarious and, at times, perilous undertaking. Clearly, this cultural mentality produces serious matters for consideration by church courts.

When one enters a marriage with a defective intention against the permanence or perpetuity of the marriage bond, he contracts marriage invalidly. For instance, "I will marry you

only if I can leave at some future date and marry someone else."
Or, more realistically, "I consent to marry you providing I can
divorce you if the marriage proves to be unhappy or
disastrous." This person has entered an invalid marriage. To
have this situation verified, the person with defective intention
must consent to the right to a lasting marriage.

The nature of perpetuity and permanence is such that it
enters into the basic definition of what marriage is in its
essence. To intend to enter a marriage with a view to the right
to divorce at a later time is not to give the spouse the right to a
lasting, perpetual union. One's mental outlook can be such that
he or she believes in permanent marriage, only if the union
works out — otherwise divorce is in order. This strikes at the
heart of our christian understanding of the nature of marriage
and, therefore, given the above attitude a marriage contracted
therefrom can be annulled.

If you have become involved in such a marriage, please
contact your tribunal for assistance. While the grounds here
spoken of can be most complicated and intricate, nevertheless,
this does not mean you will be unable to prove your case.
Particular notice should be paid to this ground since today
numerous young marriages are being contracted under these
conditions outlined. There is no surefire guarantee against
marrying someone with a defective intention. However, if you
suspect that your spouse never intended to remain married to
you for life, bring your story to the church court. It is the only
way you will ever know for certain about your chance or
prospects for a church annulment.

CONCLUSION

The foregoing has been an attempt to enlighten the reading
public on the various grounds for annulment in the church
today, as well as briefly explaining the meaning and function of
tribunals in the church. To be sure, many who read this book

will quickly recognize in their own conjugal life elements which could pass for possible invalidity. However, caution must be taken when reading and assessing marriage, whether it be yours or that of a relative or friend. Caution is demanded since not every marriage is annulable, and frequently the grounds upon which a case might be built cannot be supported with the evidence necessary to grant an affirmative decision.

Yet it is today's experience, particularly in America, that most of those petitioning for a church annulment usually obtain a favorable decision. As we mentioned earlier, this must not lead to false optimism since disappointment in this area can be profound and bitter. While the church has grown in her overall understanding of what marriage is and in what the necessary elements demanded for validity consist, nevertheless, the church is not in the business of running "divorce mills" or "annulment factories." No one can hope to slip a case by the tribunal with little or no effort, cooperation and honesty. The church has always and, will continue to scrupulously monitor marriage and annulment, for family life must be preserved, fostered and strengthened.

The church realizes that many people become enmeshed in marriages which were never valid in the eyes of God and his church. It is to these facts the tribunal ministers and for these faithful that the church courts were founded. This is not to say that marriage work is the only work for tribunals, but only that essentially, at least today, most of a tribunal's workday, week and year is taken up with the annulment proceedings.

There are those voices both in and outside the church which would have you believe that there is no need for tribunals. All that need be done, they say, is to declare the union dead and start again. To these people we respond — you are sadly mistaken. For while the church courts still have a great deal to do and much further development is necessary in order to more adequately meet the needs of our faithful and insure swift justice, this does not argue for the uselessness of tribunal structures. People need official approval for remarriage. This need exists apart from the church's laws. It is a basic psychological need to have official approbation for action which seems somehow to be visserally out of order. That is to say, people marry in order to stay together for life, raise a family and share love. When the ideal fails, it brings upon one a feeling of insecurity which leads to self-doubt and guilt. What the advocates of "carte blanche" separation and divorce without church intervention fail to realize is, that their philosophy is psychologically hollow and produces more guilt and insecurity than if the person faced up to the dilemma in the church.

For too long now the average person has known nothing of the breakthrough in the annulment procedure. Most still believe that once married, however dreadful or perhaps invalid, that nothing can be done to help them after the union comes tumbling down. The purpose of this book is to bring the laity and clergy up to date on just where annulment now stands and the rights of people to a hearing. Not to know is not to be helped.

May those who finding themselves in a broken marriage, upon reading this book, be inspired to have their lives set aright in the church through a tribunal review of their case. May those reading this book who have relatives and friends involved in marital failure pass along the information contained herein. Then perhaps others in need of help may find in the church's courts the justice they thought themselves denied, and in finding justice, discover the rewards of perseverance and peace.

APPENDIX

I. CONJUGAL COVENANT: A NEW LOOK AT AN OLD INSTITUTION

An honest consideration of the subject of marriage requires that the attitudes and behavior of the young married be examined. There is a decided shift in attitude and values on the part of the young persons entering marriage. Yet this shift represents a duality of attitude that exists in the church and society, for while the current state of marriage is lamentably impoverished, and divorce the order of the day, hope breaks on the matrimonial horizon in the form of a true, yet primitive, spiritualism which is clearly evidenced in the thinking and behavior of our young men and women.

A concern with material things can be accorded a persuasive place in contemporary marriage and is at once understandable though the source of much sorrow. In a society whose goals appear to be upward mobility and status, material concern remains a high priority. Furthermore, inflation is forcing the country to be even more conscious of money and its enlightened use. Yet, to be unconcerned about one's financial future, especially in a situation that involves marriage and family, would be irresponsible. But here's the rub: money and gainful employment ought always to be pursued as a means to further the higher values of love. We must not only do the right things, but we must do them for the right reasons.

This attitude of using the created goods of the earth and the wages we merit from honest employment to further the gospel values of love and fidelity is in harmony with the biblical notion of the poverty of spirit. Wealth is not at issue here, only the proper use of one's good fortune and the gospel generosity which leads to a proper detachment from earthly gains. It is this search for freedom from earthly entrapment which has sparked the spiritual movements that have risen within the last two decades.

A compelling sense of individual freedom, its absolute value both in a properly secular society and the spiritual community (St. Paul's Letter to the Galatians) has produced the awareness that true freedom is bought at a great price — one of the costs is excessive material concern. The young people of the 1960's, inspired as they were (and are) by the influence of existentialism and personalism, have concluded that money, status, and position are important, yet to cling to them at all costs is a perilous enterprise.

The experience of the 60's not only touched the youth of that time, but dramatically affected the entire culture, producing such things as charismatic renewal, consultation in decision making, passionate concern for the issues of war and peace, environmental protection, and racial injustice, among many other items. The reaction to the Vietnam War and the pollution crisis are but two examples of the shift toward a more ethically and spiritually sensitized culture. Likewise, the opposition against misguided expenditures for war, armaments and space programs, in the face of dire poverty indicates a shift in how the people are now viewing the use of material gains. This indicates a growing movement — admittedly at an infant stage — toward the biblical understanding of poverty and wealth. Nor can an observer ignore the phenomenon known as the "hippies." Their very life style is a clear indication of the quest for the spiritual values of (biblical) poverty and justice that seem to be present and growing within our society.

Along about the 1960's youth began to search for the lost values of life and love, which had been hidden from their experience by unsuspecting parents who inadvertently developed an attitude of "business as usual" relative to the home life. What was happening at this time is simply this: the culture began to change at the hands of a shift in socio-cultural thinking and the political economic forces at work within the society. Values were questioned against a background of relative inflexibility. This gave way to a credibility gap as those institutions, which in the past had upheld societal principles, began to lose control of their own credibility. The accusation of hypocrisy was then leveled at them and the young started to search for contemporary values apart from the institution.

Linked to this critical situation the Catholic Church began a program of religious renewal at the hands of John XXIII. Hence, youth discovered biblical values and while their understanding of these values suffered from lack of contact with the Christian heritage, nonetheless, they grasped at these values and began their own interpretation of how these values applied to modern man.

How did this affect marriage? Clearly, marriage had been linked with the "old school" institution and pervaded by "old school" values, (which, by the way, were not all bad). Consequently, those of marital age during this time and even yet, felt compelled to introduce their own newly discovered ethos into their particular matrimonial philosophy. The sexual dimension, clearly integral to married life, found a secondary place in this philosophy. While the youth felt that sex was good and beautiful and adequately expressed their inner commitment, they still felt compelled to establish the priority of interpersonal relationship and community of life.

Perhaps the sexual mores which attend to this approach to marriage are questionable but what has motivated the commune type living reflects a deeper understanding of the lasting and significant value of interpersonal communion. If one were to ask whether or not this commune type life style will survive the acid test of time and history, I would answer resoundingly in the negative. But the spark which has inspired the experiment will surely lead to a deep vision of marriage and family life. Once the value of permanence and stability are recognized with reference to marriage and the truth of common life begins to course through conjugal veins, then we will have moved in the direction of revaluing and reconstructing the "institution" of marriage in terms of modern man.

It can be verified with at least some assuredness that our youth are beginning to put off marriage until they feel secure and ready to settle down. The young married finds today's world a perilous field in which to take root. It is most difficult to begin commune life and love amidst the problems which beset the growing family. But in spite of the times, which often work against stability in marriage, young people are finding their own way and their own direction despite prophets of doom.

The reserving of a late age to covenant themselves signals a more enlightened approach to the seriousness of marriage and a deep understanding of the realities confronting modern man. One point to be noted here is that the impetus to continue one's education after high school and even post-graduate work has extended the period of adolescence into the middle 20's. Since schooling implies a dependency it seems logical to conclude that one is not set for marriage (generally) until the middle twenties. Surely, this was not the case in the past. Youth today mature slower and later than in previous generations, but their maturity, once achieved, is sharper, more astute and more enlightened to realities, and generally more in tune with the cultural situation of the day. Let us not, however, submit to the besetting temptation to equate *older* with *mature* because this can be erroneous and misleading.

Disturbing, however, is the present indication that young people are less willing to be long suffering than their previous constituents. This is at once healthy and perilous. It is healthy because it reflects a thinking which says, "I will not put up with unreasonable and intolerable situations for the sake of saving face, or because others expect this of me, or because I am told to do so. I must do what I must in order to be a totally integrated person and contribute to those around me the fruits of my talents, energies, and God given personality." This drive toward self-actualization and self-determination is not a cause for alarm but a signal that personhood is being respected and the sense of personal responsibility is being acknowledged.

This country was founded on such high ideals and the gospel experience ratifies the all-important value of following your conscience and in not burying your talents, nor hiding your light under a "bushel basket." It appears that through all the accusations of religionlessness, or valuelessness, there has never been greater cause to hope than we have today. At no time in history has the value of life and love been so esteemed as in our time.

Even despite the fact that the contraception issue has become somewhat moot, and abortional practices are more widespread today, still the underlying values of life and love remain firm through it all. It is our youth who support pro-life philosophies, either the pro-life movement per se, or implicitly via a dedication to environmental protection, conscientious objection and the poverty issue. The vital signs of our people have never been so strong even though many sins are being committed in the name of love.

From the youth experience of the 1960's comes the women's liberation question. This involves the issue we have already addressed and signals the overriding determination, on the part of our young nation, to respect personhood and the right to freedom and self-determination, even if this involves a certain degree of possible danger. Women are no longer ready nor willing to be used by society, and one suspects that in the not too distant future very few women will be "taken advantage of, sexually," or submit sexually, unless there be a degree of love involved. The same, of course, holds true for the man.

In the past, sexual liberty has taken its toll on the sexual relationship which is intrinsic to conjugal love. It has weakened the beauty of physical expression for those who have so abused it and has exhausted for them its divine meaning. This is a problem of the ages and does not submit to facile resolution. However, today, while indeed sexual abuses and double standards abound, still we sense the movement away from such purely physical "love" towards a more integrated concept of the place physical expression holds within the matrimonial covenant. No longer is the "marriage debt" solely a duty, but it is understood as the most significant expression of genuine marital love. Sex and love are inseparable from their authentic meaning. When each is considered apart from the other, they lose their true meaning and value. This, I believe, the youth movement of the decade has conveyed to us in its own and admittedly at times, cruel way. But the foundational potential for a positive and enlightened understanding of genuine marriage reality has been laid. It now remains for all of us to fashion this new viewpoint into a genuine Judeo-Christian value. Summarizing all that has been said into a conclusion is a most difficult and at times arduous task. Dare we even attempt? Yet the poetry of life demands expression and who are we to deny our poets their message. In many unique ways the renewed emphasis on life and love has come to us in poetic language, song, and art form. These are the pristine ways in which man expresses himself. While the poets take liberties accorded no one else, and perhaps because they can do so, they convey the dreams and depths of the human heart and the goals of youth.

The future of marriage is in the hands of the young. It is in a real sense in our hands. It is and always will be in the hands of God for the Spirit blows where it will, and through all the clouds and confusion surrounding contemporary marriage, there lurks beautifully, salvifically, the grace of God, which surpasses human understanding, and ultimately leads lovers to homecoming.

II. PREPARING COUPLES FOR MARRIAGE: A NEW PERSPECTIVE

There is much discussion these days concerning the preparation of couples for their future marital union. Both at the provincial level and, to a larger but more general extent, at the level of professional societies, such as the Canon Law Society of America, the arresting question of how and to what extent the church must properly prepare young persons for marriage is being seriously considered.

The pre-marital investigation which the church, in theory, takes most seriously has been conducted by way of custom in a very *pro forma* manner. This is due in large part to the many outdated and unrealistic questions proposed in the pre-nuptial questionnaire. While some questions are to the point and the proper documentation indispensible, others are of dubious value at best. The time has come to revaluate and reformulate our pre-nuptial investigation process and to begin asking some very pertinent questions which reflect the cultural condition in America.

Before presenting those areas of investigation which are in need of discussion and elucidation, let us set the context for our analysis by way of some background.

Perhaps the overriding consideration when attempting a discussion on the causes of marital failure and its possible prevention by way of preparation is to mark out the root cause — that of ignorance. Most marital failures result from ignorance and its offshoots: fear and distrust. The less we know about someone the greater the probability for our future alienation from him. Our distance from another is directly proportional to our ignorance of him as a person: ignorance of his beliefs and hopes; his dreams and difficulties; his joys and sorrows; his past mistakes and present interests.

Who Am I Marrying?

It seems that in America, people generally marry with less

knowledge about the personhood of their partner and the understanding surrounding that which they are about to undertake, than they possess when purchasing something in a store. The experts in the fields of social psychology relate to us that their studies indicate almost one-half of all marriages attempted last year will end in personal and social disaster. In California the percentages are even higher. If America is indeed the unhappy leader in the field of marital discord, as the facts appear to indicate, then the acceptable time for doing something about this condition is upon us.

Some unsettling and arresting questions remain unresolved: What is wrong with a system of values and attitudes that will allow the richest, most educated nation on earth the liberty of basking in so dubious an honor? What has gone awry in a society which allows its people the lamentable joy of impermanence? Why does America paint so ugly a picture of so beautiful a relationship? Why do people so quickly ask out of that for which they worked so long getting into? Is life as absurd as all this seems to demonstrate? Is love a fleeting experience which defines itself in terms of a temporary commitment?

Perhaps if marriage were to be made more difficult to get into, instead of getting out of, it would drive home the seriousness of the commitment involved. This posture might give one pause before jumping at the chance to enter a relationship that terminates only in death. What if we required a certain degree of mutual knowledge as a prerequisite for entering upon a life-long commitment, would there then be the number of dissolutions we presently see? For instance, if couples planning marriage were obliged to investigate their motives for marrying each other and the obligations ensuing from such a relationship, it is solidly probable that many would choose not to marry this particular partner.

Current studies cite the following reasons for much of the trouble marriages encounter: 1). The pressures of modern society. 2). The urban crisis. 3). The nuclear age and its corollaries. 4). The overriding mood of permissiveness. 5). The smashing of traditional mores. 6). The contemporary financial burdens and so on. Now, while most professional counselors insist that such a battery of problems may and can aggravate already existing marital difficulties, they equally insist that they are not the root causes of marital discord. Instead we find these realities being dragged into existing relationships as so much excess baggage. This should not astonish us; it has always been a fact of life.

Marriage today is no more joyless than it has ever been. What creates today's rise in unhappiness and discontent is people's increasing unwillingness to settle for such a sad state of affairs. People quite dissatisfied with their marriages are less likely today to be long-suffering. Of course through all of this the recurring problem of personal ignorance stands alone as the root cause of joylessness. The intensity of joylessness is proportional to the rise in misunderstanding and lack of proper communication in any given marriage. Ignorance spawns misunderstanding which is the result of lost communication. Ignorance of each other's views on life and love and a variety of related topics is key to marital trouble. Ignorance breeds fear and distrust which are the usual causes for separation and divorce.

How does a couple cancel such ignorance? People cancel ignorance by informing one another concerning those areas of life and love which touch directly upon their married lives and the hopes they possess for a realizable future. Let's discuss some of the practical, gutsy categories that affect marriages but are seldom touched upon in current matrimonial preparation. Let us perhaps attach these questions in the manner of an agenda to the current pre-nuptial questionnaire:

Is Money the Problem

His salary: What is the annual income of your fiancé? Does

it serve to satisfy his needs at present and will it (given increments) serve to allow fulfillment of his hopes and dreams for your future together? But more importantly, are you, his bride-to-be, really content to live on that salary and the level of social status which it creates, and do so for the rest of your life? Are you really content with this? Will his financial status allow you to function socially as you feel you must and still be capable of educating your children, and at the same time live in relative comfort? Honesty here is a grave necessity.

What if at some future date your spouse is called upon to support his or her parents. Will you accept this policy with the warmth and love that gave it birth or rather will this eat away at your feelings and needs concerning "cutting loose those apron strings," therefore spawning resentment: "I wish he were as concerned for me!"

The In-Laws: Suppose Mr. X is extraordinarily close to his parents and requires constant visitation in order to be "true" to his love for them. Or perhaps his parents are the ones who insist upon his continual and frequent visitation. Can Miss Y cope with this situation? Has it been discussed and agreed upon? What if one or both of his or her parents fall sick or one dies; will either refuse to allow the parent involved to move in with them? How strongly do you feel about this prospect?

What Priorities Prevail?

Now suppose, for instance, Miss Y visits her widowed mother two or three times weekly and has done so for a number of years running. Or possibly Miss Y still lives home. Both she and her mother require this presence. How will this situation affect the prospects of moving to a new location away from the mother? For example, her husband's job requires such a move and he is opposed to "mother" moving along with them. What priorities are operative here? Is compromise an essential? If so, how far does one go in compromising his position on such matters?

Abortion: Here lies a potential battlefield; also a classic example of the destruction following upon ignorance. Take for instance the fact Miss Y has had an abortion due to illegitimacy and fails to tell her fiance of this unfortunate occurrence prior to marriage. The reason she fails to mention the tragedy results from embarrassment and shame. Or perhaps worse still the fiance has indicated his outrageous hostility to such practices and has further announced that he despises such women. Upon discovering such awful knowledge he reacts with disgust and revulsion toward her. This can quickly precipitate divorce.

When a couple contemplating marriage begins to talk seriously of the future, the question of abortion as a means to eliminate an unwanted pregnancy should have a high priority on the list of topics to be discussed. If either one of the two agrees that this is, or could become, a necessary way out of a supposed dilemma, then the seeds for future turmoil exist and chances are they could be sown. If sharp discord concerning an abortion is evident then their marriage, quite simply, is a potential disaster. A second look at this marriage's prospects in light of this issue is imperative.

Residence: This question is an important one, and while it is discussed by most couples, oftentimes it is not fully investigated. The couple about to be married agree that city Z will be their residence. Here is where they will settle and it is here where their children will grow up. However, your husband's employment may require, at some future moment (after you are already settled), moving to another state or even to another country. Will your initial agreement on the location of residence still remain the same? Has some ignorance of feeling and values remained unsaid prior to marriage? It appears the agreement which can abide and insure tranquility in this area is the agreement on the part of the wife that she will go anywhere her husband's job takes them, and do so unreservedly. No other attitude will assure a minimum of difficulty should such an occasion arise.

Religious Beliefs: If agreement cannot be reached along these lines then, like politics, discussion with this area of life can prove to be distressing at best. If one of the parties is religious, can he tolerate the irreligious life style of the other? Will their divergent points of view affect the religious upbringing of the children? Will either interfere with the other's conscience as it touches upon the question of religion? Will the disbelieving partner ridicule the beliefs of the other? If so, can this be done to such an extent that their love becomes permanently wounded? How will all of this affect the children?

If religion is an integral part of life, as experience seems to indicate, then its relation to a marriage is certainly a question that needs to be addressed.

The Working Wife: If in the light of women's liberation Miss Y decided after the birth of her child that she will return to work, what effect will this position have on the marriage given the husband's insistence upon her being home with the kids? Since so many of today's women are college graduates and therefore presumably are looking for an outlet by which to exercise their knowledge and skill, how will this attitude square with the traditional notion of family life? If this matter is not settled definitely prior to contracting marriage, then the inevitability of crisis cannot be avoided. The problem is heightened considerably if the husband's financial status does not require his wife's working.

Should We Adopt?

Adoption: Take this case in point: both parties desire to have children but for some reason she cannot seem to get pregnant. What then? Assuming fertility existed for both parties prior to the marriage, one's initial course of action would be to determine the cause of this unfortunate sterility. After consultation with a physician (or psychologist) the couple discovers that, in fact, a case of sterility exists. How will the marriage hold up upon learning of this situation? No one knows for certain. But what is certain is that the couple who thought it necessary to discuss this vital question will be able to deal with the situation more rationally.

Therefore, the question of adoption arises. She wants children but he refuses to "take in somebody else's child." "If we can't have our own then we'll have none." The tension is apparent. Once again, unless this question has been cleared up before marriage, the possibility of disaster resulting from this problem becomes a reality for the couple. Since sterility can be visited upon any marriage at any time, the adoption question simply must be agreed upon before a contract takes place. Not to do so will insure a state of ignorance, and such ignorance can return to haunt marriage and perhaps destroy it altogether. The question: If sterility becomes a reality for us, will we adopt?

Vacations Are Important

Vacation and Family Recreation: Ignorance within this area of marital life is not to be taken lightly. Most working men and women live from vacation to vacation. They save frugally from week to week and plan intensely for vacation as the year speeds along its appointed course. Vacation seems to instill within a marriage some sort of sanity and joy. It offers a well-deserved break for those who have worked hard in the salt mines of life. It isn't a panacea for all problems, but it certainly enables one to see the difficulties in a far more comfortable and relaxed light.

Now, everyone has his own peculiar ideas about how a vacation should be spent, or exactly what a vacation is or even should be. Given such variety of personal opinion, and given the context of marriage, there flows a need for necessary flexibility on the part of the partners that allows for mutual agreement. Aside from the difficulty of coordinating such a venture, what problems are likely to result from ignorance in the area of one's vacation?

1). *Young Children:* Should young children be dragged, say to the shore, where every year countless toddlers are badly sunburned and require hospitalization? Likewise, many children have their eyesight permanently damaged from sand in the eyes. Perhaps, then, your children will determine the place for your vacation. This should be discussed by couples: What will we do in terms of vacation while our children are still young?

2). *Type of Vacation:* What is a vacation for one person is hell for another. What is a vacation for a wife is not for her husband. What is a vacation for children is not for their parents. How does a resident grandmother or grandfather affect your family's vacation plans? These and other vital questions must be dealt with by the couple, ideally before marriage.

What exactly is each partner looking for from his or her vacation? How will both of their needs be best served? If a vacation is not a vacation for all, it is a vacation for none.

Hobby Or Hubby?

Hobbies: Another vital outlet for recreation and relaxation is a hobby. It allows and provides a means for creativity and personal satisfaction. The sad fact is that some hobbies work against a marriage rather than support it. Some hobbies demand more time and, I dare say, more love than is given to one's spouse. Some hobbies are not compatible with another living under the same roof. They have prerequisite conditions necessary for their proper fulfillment. In many cases the spouse may be directly affected and therefore should be agreeable to the hobby. The needs of the spouse must be taken into account when considering a prospective hobby. If, for instance, a particular wife requires the loving presence of her husband and her husband's hobby is hunting and fishing, one which takes him away frequently (oftentimes during holiday seasons), then perhaps his hobby could be the cause of resentment. It is likely, therefore, that she will belittle his hobby. If this hobby is extremely important to him (perhaps overly so) her belittling might ignite a full-scale marital war.

Eliminate confusion: The same applies with regard to her hobbies. It seems that if trouble is to be avoided, one's spouse must be in some way involved with the other's hobby, however remotely that might be. Ignorance and insensitivity here, coupled with a dose of non-communication, is a source for numerous aggravations and discord.

I have attempted to outline just some of the less-talked-about areas within married life which can lead to domestic discord if not properly understood and reasoned out together. Very often estrangement and alienation begin with confusion over these simple elements that constitute the vitality of marriage because they require the life-giving ingredient — communication. Adequate understanding in the aforementioned areas of married life will help sustain a lasting personal relationship. The motives for which one enters marriage should be scrupulously analyzed and reflected upon before attempting a long-term commitment. Nothing but honesty will suffice.

III. PETITION FOR AN ECCLESIASTICAL ANNULMENT
(Formal Process)

PLEASE ANSWER THE FOLLOWING QUESTIONS COMPLETELY AND
HONESTLY, BE ASSURED THAT THE INFORMATION YOU SUPPLY WILL BE
HELD IN THE STRICTEST PROFESSIONAL CONFIDENCE, TO BE USED ONLY
FOR THE PURPOSE OF ECCLESIASTICAL ANNULMENT PROCEEDINGS.

Name _____ Age _____
    (if woman, include maiden name)
Address _____ Phone _____
Date of Birth _____ Place of birth _____
Religion _____ Are you baptized? . . . _____ Yes _____ No

REGARDING YOUR PREVIOUS MARRIAGE:

1. Name of the person you married _____
2. His/her present address _____
                    (Street, City and State)
3. When did your previous marriage take place?
                            (Month, Day and Year)
4. Where did it take place? _____
                    (Church, City and State)
5. What is the religion of your former spouse? _____
            Was he/she baptized? _____ Yes _____No
6. If so, when and where? _____
7. Were children born of the union? ... _____ Yes _____ No
8. Are you now living apart? .... _____ Yes _____ No
9. Date of the final separation _____
10. In your own words, explain in detail why the marriage failed.
    _____
    _____

11. Has either party to the marriage ever sought or obtained
professional help, psychiatric or psychological, before,
during, or after the marriage? .... _____ Yes _____ No
If so, which party? _____
Please supply the doctors' names and addresses that we might

contact them for their expert testimony, and enclose a signed release, properly notarized.

---

12. Has a civil divorce, or annulment, been obtained ?

    ＿＿Yes ＿＿No

    If so, which one? ＿＿＿＿＿＿＿＿＿＿＿＿＿＿＿＿

        When? ＿＿＿＿＿＿＿＿＿＿＿＿＿＿＿＿＿＿

            (Month, Day, Year)

        Where? ＿＿＿＿＿＿＿＿＿＿＿＿＿＿＿＿＿

            (City and State)

        On what grounds? ＿＿＿＿＿＿＿＿＿＿＿＿＿

13. Keeping in mind that an ecclesiastical annulment means the marriage was invalid from the beginning and, therefore, never a sacramental union in God's sight, do you think the Catholic Church should annul your marriage?＿＿Yes ＿＿No

    If so, on what basis? ＿＿＿＿＿＿＿＿＿＿＿＿＿＿＿

---

14. Was the marriage in question contracted freely and with mutual love? .... ＿＿Yes ＿＿No

    If not, please explain, in detail, giving circumstances leading up to the marriage. ＿＿＿＿＿＿＿＿＿＿＿＿＿＿＿

---

15. Was there any force or fear used by anyone (threats, physical harm, etc.) to make either party marry? .. ＿＿Yes ＿＿No

    Please explain in detail ＿＿＿＿＿＿＿＿＿＿＿＿＿＿

---

16. In contracting this marriage, did you and your spouse intend a permanent, lifelong union, binding until death? ＿＿Yes ＿＿No

    If not, please explain completely the intentions on this point.

---

17. In contracting this marriage, did either party have any serious doubts about its successful and happy outcome? Please explain in detail............................... ＿＿Yes ＿＿No

---

18. Was there an agreement, or unilateral intention, about getting
a divorce if the marriage proved unhappy? ____Yes ____No
Was this agreement prior to the marriage? ____Yes ____No
Are there any witnesses to this agreement? ____Yes ____No
If so, please list the names and addresses: _____

_____

19. Did either of you make any statements shortly after the
marriage about a divorce? ....____Yes ____No
If so, please elaborate in detail _____

_____

20. In entering this marriage did you both intend to have children?

_____

21. Prior to the marriage, did either of you state that you would
not have children? _____
Was this exclusion to be temporary or permanent?_____
What was the reason given for excluding children?_____

_____

Are there any witnesses to these statements? ____Yes ____No
If so, please list the names and addresses: _____

22. Was anything said or done after the marriage to indicate
that either of you did not intend to have children?   ____

_____

_____

23. In entering this marriage, did you both intend to be sexually
faithful only to each other for life? _____

_____

24. Prior to the marriage, did either of you lay down some
condition? For example, "I will only if, or provided that."
If so, please explain fully.......................... ____Yes ____No

_____

_____

25. Have you entered into a new marriage? ...... ____Yes ____No
If so, please give the following information:
Name of the person you married _____

Date of the marriage _____ Place _____
Officiating Witness _____

26. Have you previously presented a petition for annulment to this Tribunal or any other Tribunal? ...._____Yes _____No
If so, please give the approximate date and name of the Tribunal._____

27. IMPORTANT AND NECESSARY:

   Please include along with this petition the following information:

   1. A detailed account of your relationship to your spouse, prior to marriage (especially the engagement period), during marriage, and up to and including the final breakup. *Include all facts*, however insignificant.
   2. Have this account of your marriage *notarized.*
   3. Include divorce decree and ask your lawyer to supply copies of the full acts of the divorce proceedings.
   4. Names and addresses of any and all persons who can act as witnesses or shed some light on your presentation of the facts.

28. Do you swear to the truth of all your statements? _____

   Date: _____   _____
                                              signature

   Referred by _____

IV. CANON LAW AND SECOND MARRIAGES

Within recent years there has been much publicity given to resolving certain marriage cases, involving a second marriage, by using the "good conscience" solution. It frequently happens that people who truly deserve a Church annulment of a past marriage that failed, cannot receive one because of a lack of evidence: witnesses have died, or will not cooperate, or cannot be located, to take a few examples. A careful assessment of all the alleged facts is taken into consideration by the tribunal, together with a firm desire to meet the demands of justice in the best possible way. Accordingly, many tribunal priests have guided such unfortunate petitioners back to a conscientious reception of the sacraments, even though it remains impossible for the church to acknowledge the validity of their present marriages "on the record."

A few dioceses around the country attempted to formalize these actions taken in good faith in the private realm of conscience by making such procedures new "laws" to be observed throughout their territories. The reaction was not long in coming, and proved to be quite disapproving on the part of the higher Church authorities. It was felt that those dioceses had exceeded the limits of legitimate authority, even admitting the inadequacies of present canon law with the Church marriage laws.

As an institution, canon law has remained relatively unknown to the average Catholic layman except in that single area which frequently touches his personal life most intimately: marriage law. The laity's unfamiliarity with the role of canon law in the life of the Church should not strike anyone as particularly surprising, since the Code of Canon Law is, by and large, concerned primarily with the clerical side of the Church. One would logically presume, therefore, that most habitual criticisms upon this controversial institution are perpetrated principally by bishops, priests, and seminarians. Their lives, after all, are affected directly by canonical statutes in every respect.

Constructive criticism is not to be deplored. On the contrary, given the patent inadequacies of the present Code, it is welcome. What is alarming, however, is the extent to which large segments of the clergy have increasingly tended to disregard the proper role and function of law in the life of the visible Church. By failing to distinguish between an imperfect statute and the purpose for which that statute exists, a simplistic approach to life in the Church has emerged which the present sophisticated development of Church structure quite simply cannot sustain.

Now it is clearly absurd to visualize the Church, after twenty centuries of human, cultural, sociological, and technological advance, as ideally defined to the world it must serve in order to justify its existence in the primitive style of its infant organization. The gospel ideal and ethic for which early Christians shed their blood remains constant, but it must be accommodated to corresponding human development.

As long as men remain human beings, a human structure will always be necessary to "capture" that divine and creative Spirit who gives to man the really convincing "explanation" for his own existence and inspires him to nobility of purpose and action. Historically, crises have arisen when the structure no longer reflected the Spirit which gave it viability. Due always to human failing, it sought to contain and stifle the free movements proper to divine inspiration.

V. CANON LAW'S STRUCTURE-CRISIS

Human structures, whether political or ecclesiastical, always seem to have been characterized by a "built-in" reluctance to change or to accommodate themselves in the face of newly evolving cultural patterns. Therefore, when values and behavior patterns reflect new ways of perceiving old realities, institutions ordinarily determine that their existence is threatened and react accordingly. The avant-garde usually completes the polarization of issues around which the crisis is revolving simply by challenging the older and more established perspective, which the institution reflects, with its own brilliant and highly suspect vision. In the presentation of new ideas, an avant-garde group frequently tends to dismiss the existing institution as "hopelessly outdated," an implicit accusation that the structure is inherently *incapable* of the desired modifications. The threatened institution on the other hand tends to consider the new vision as radical, "far-out," and therefore impossible for purposes of assimilation. The establishment and the avant-garde seldom trust each other sufficiently to do the obvious: acknowledge the aspects of enduring validity which characterize the former, while assimilating the more relevant, and perhaps more truthful, expressions of permanent values which bring the latter into periodic existence.

The aforementioned structure-crisis exists today in canon law. The 20th century Church has become, over centuries of development, a highly sophisticated assembly of believers. Such refined development necessitates the proper subordinated role of the Church law within its institutional framework precisely in order to maintain that stability which will lend credibility to the Church's overall mission of bringing the light of the gospel to all nations. Such an exalted goal cannot be achieved by burying one's head in the sand and refusing to see the essential need for Church order in the form of appropriate legislation. Neither is one justified in pointing the finger at glaring insufficiencies in our present code of law, and then attempting to "solve" the problem by a call to abolish the structure of law totally from the everyday life of the Church. This unwarranted and utterly simplistic "solution" cannot be based on some vague appeal to the "simple" structure of the church in the first centuries of development, together with the claim that such a primitive Church knew no legal system such as we have today. Of course it didn't! But neither did the Church know the structural development then that manifests its presence to the world today. As a matter of fact, the primitive Church did sanction a Church-order, and it did, most assuredly, invoke human prescriptions to regulate in an orderly way the lives of Church members.

VI. THE REFORM OF THE CODE

It is difficult at this point to state clearly in which direction the present reform of canon law is going. Initiated originally under the auspices of Pope John XXIII, the commission responsible for the new Code of Canon Law has shrouded its work in such a secrecy that one can be justified in pessimism. It would seem that unless the canon lawyers in Europe and the United States, who are currently propounding a more enlightened jurisprudence in many areas of Church law, and most emphatically in the area of marriage, are allowed to join sympathetic forces with the Code Commission in a genuine effort of mutual trust and cooperation, the new Code might very well serve only to compel the choosing of sides, thereby fostering a permanent polarization of mind and attitude.

Even though American canonists today are writing and publishing their own reflections in that area of law which treats of Christian marriage, it seems that insufficient time is being allowed for the evolved jurisprudence to reach genuine fruition. Ideas that seek to challenge the accepted axioms of centuries need to be expressed in many various ways and discussed freely by competent scholars over a protracted period. When one stops to consider that a new and "revised" Code of Canon Law might very well make its appearance within the next five years, the conclusion is almost certain that the section dealing with marriage will still not reveal a treatment that can be called adequate for our time.

Although certain inadequacies of current matrimonial
legislation are apparent to Diocesan Tribunals, it would be
tragically simplistic for laymen to fault the institution of
Canon Law exclusively when marital discord arises. We
humans are usually unwilling to assume the burdens imposed
by our own sense of guilt. A scapegoat is sought out, almost
instinctively, upon which the shock and deep hurt that result
from a marriage failure can be placed. The contemporary crisis
that plagues the structure of law in the Church presents itself as
a most convenient victim which to an unreflective mind will
serve to alleviate merited guilt that results from either (a) the
personal moral failings of basically selfish spouses who seek
their own interests only, or (b) the incompetence of certain
canon lawyers who remain inflexible regarding certain legal
positions developed over a long period of time. These
positions, hopelessly inadequate if not unjust, are imposed as
"solutions" to delicate cases again and again, all in the name of
a "fidelity" to the laws of the Church. When the inadequacies
become apparent to them in the lives of the people presumably
being "served," there are no self-indictments forthcoming.
There are only impersonal accusations brought against "that
ol' devil," canon law.

Many restless and dissatisfied priests in other areas of
Church work today make use of the same rationalization
rather than face honestly their own failings and shortcomings
as ministers of Christ. In other words, one cannot validly
substitute the liabilities presently built into some of our legal
concepts and procedures for a deeply personal inability or
unwillingness to accept the full implications and consequences
of one's moral decisions in life. It is of little consequence and
even less satisfying to possess an honestly enlightened
jurisprudence regarding Christian marriage if spouses
themselves fail to reflect a maturely developed commitment to
faith. Both are absolutely essential for a balanced perspective

in arriving at an eventual solution to institutional and personal crises.

VII. ACCEPTING THE GOSPEL'S IDEAL

In its ethical understanding of the gospel, the Roman Church has always proposed the ideal for her sons and daughters. In the past this idealism usually afforded even hardened critics of the Church an opportunity to voice sentiments of admiration. Today, however, the phenomenon has made its appearance on the Church scene that not only doubts the usefulness of maintaining an ideal expression of the gospel but even questions the validity of such proposals. One might presume that such rejection of Christian ideals is largely the result of a current obsession in many quarters of the post-conciliar Church to address the word in terms that are relevant to, supposedly, the world's understanding of itself. Some go even further, and suggest that if the Church is not speaking to the world with an effective degree of relevance, the fault belongs with the Church, which, they advise, should be corrected, even at the expense of Christian idealism. This view, unfortunately for those Christians who expound it, cannot be reconciled with either scriptural or theological expressions of the Church's divine mission to reconcile an alienated world to God, principally through the death and resurrection of Christ. It is the revelation of Christ that judges earthly values and assigns to them a validity proportionate to Christian existence. Life in Christ can never be made to hinge on conformity to a value system previously unassessed in the light of God's redemptive activity on behalf of mankind.

The Church must continue, therefore, to preach and uphold Christian life formulated according to its ideal expression. At the same time it must strive to assist each member to attain the realization of that ideal through a charitable assimilation of the frail human condition to the saving likeness of Christ. The Church cannot afford to settle for anything less than Christ's vision of marriage, regardless of any amount of outside pressure to abandon, however slightly, such a vision in the name of "relevance." The Church will thus remain faithful to the Word of God, even in the face of warranted legal criticism directed to the human ecclesiastical expression of that very ideal so highly prized.

One might legitimately ponder at this point the problem of how unhappy spouses can, in the present "crisis-interim," retain the utmost fidelity to ideal faith when confronted by a distressing inability of the Church to render needed assistance in virtue of lagging matrimonial legislation. Two Christians might have entered a second marriage upon the sincere conscientious conviction that the previous marriage of one of them was invalid. Perhaps the invalidity stemmed from a defect already acknowledged in canon law but which lacks proof in the external forum of the Church.[1] On the other hand, the reason for alleging invalidity might not have been acceptable to, or even developed in, canonical tradition in the past; now it may be evolving to an accepted status in ecclesiastical jurisprudence. The full development of this new jurisprudence, however, might not be available to the petitioner for several years hence. How can the Church be of service to him *now*, in his present need?

VIII. THE "CONSCIENCE-SOLUTION"

The canonists of the Paterson, New Jersey, Matrimonial Tribunal, were perhaps among the very first in the United States to institute in a *quasi*-official way, a practice which now has become fairly common in marriage tribunals around the country as an "interim" solution to certain marriage cases. Petitioners who were living in a second marriage, usually for a good many years, but who discovered that they were unable to prove the invalidity of the first marriage despite the solid probability that canonical grounds for a formal annulment seemed to exist, were reconciled to the sacramental life of the Church in the internal forum. Following a careful study of former marriage, the petitioner was aided, through discussions about the nature and purposes of Christian marriage, to form an upright decision in conscience as to the validity or nullity of the former union. This "decision" on the part of the petitioner then formed the basis for the "solution." If the conscience was sincerely certain that the first marriage was null, the petitioner was advised to avail himself of the sacraments, since the second marriage was solemnized in good faith, even though juridically "outside the Church."

One should not infer that the "conscience-solution" is readily applicable in the majority of cases which admit of no canonical solution in the external forum. The conscience-remedy is not interpreted as a simple acceptance by the tribunal of the fact of a second marriage. An objective basis in theology and canon law on which the probable invalidity of the first marriage is reasonably presumed, is judged to exist prior to the invocation of this "procedure." (Practically every case resolved at the Paterson tribunal in the internal forum was one in which the parties had been living in a second marriage for many years and demonstrated clearly a marital stability which also formed part of that objective basis).

The growing practice of resolving certain cases of unusual difficulty and merit in this way, commendably employed by many sensitive and learned priests of balanced perspective, has been cited principally to demonstrate one way, limited though

---

[1] The *external forum* is a legal term that connotes that "area" in the Church where public ecclesiastical recognition or avowal is given to a decision or action undertaken by a member of the Church. The *internal forum*, on the other hand, represents the realm of private conscience. The internal forum can be either sacramental (the reception of penance) or non-sacramental. Although the analogy is imperfect, the idea might best be conveyed by suggesting that if a decision or an action occurs in the internal forum, it is "off the record."

it is, in which the full fruits of our Catholic heritage can be brought to bear upon the institutional expressions of our membership in Christ, so as to render the mission of service ever more credible. Secondarily, one would always wish to hold out a vision or hope and eventual reconciliation to those Christians who truly suffer through no fault of their own in a sincere and authentic attempt to carry out the will of Christ in their own lives.

IN SUMMARY

An appeal must be made to our Christian people themselves to strive vigorously for a new awareness on their part that maturity of faith is vitally necessary to bring sacramental marriage into being and sustain it. We can reform structures, but we must, at the same time renew ourselves also. A crucial part of that authentic personal renewal will necessarily consist in a reaffirmation of faith in the absolute indissolubility of a true Christian marriage, precisely for what such a sacred reality means and stands for. The reform of canon law itself, a constantly developing theological awareness into the deeper mysteries of sacramental marriage, the simplification of procedural law in order to expedite for annulment more quickly, more justly, and more charitably, and the evolution of broader grounds for annulment, are encouraging signs of a living and relevant Church seeking to correct the inadequacies of the past.

But even with the actual realization of these reform measures, the men and women who profess a faith in Jesus Christ, and who are, for that reason, adopted children of his Father, will nevertheless be called upon by Christ to affirm for themselves in their own lives a sacred belief in the enduring nature of marriage in the Lord, a belief which can never be challenged without at the same time challenging the very Word of God upon which it rests. If Christian spouses choose to live in marriage *quo* sacrament, then they elect to make of their union a permanent manifestation of Christ's glorious victimhood to an incredulous world. A genuine reform of matrimonial law and procedures ultimately derives its real justification and sense of purpose in aiding Christians to achieve this vision of marriage, ancient in our Christian heritage, but ever new in bringing a world striving for true love to that divine fulfillment.

OTHER BOOKS FROM ALBA HOUSE

MARRIAGE TODAY: A Commentary on the Code of the Canon Law
by Bernard A. Siegle, T.O.R., J.C.D.

"It is a reliable and easy-to-use reference work. A good item
for every priest, as well as the teacher, lawyer and other
members of the laity who need to know more about marriage
regulations today." SPIRITUAL BOOK NEWS

$10.95, paper

MARRIAGE AND FAMILY: The Domestic Church
by Louis Alessio and Hector Munoz, O.P.

This book, in a very positive way, justifies the Christian
family by using the challenging analogy that the Christian is
the "domestic Church," based on a Covenant of Christ. The
author refutes those who overstress the sociological
psychological attitudes which have fostered the singles bars,
single families, single homes and single parents.

$3.95, paper

LOVE, MARRIAGE AND THE FAMILY: Yesterday and Today
by James A. Mohler, S.J.

Premarital sex, extramerital sex, divorce, etc., are threaten-
ing to destroy the structure of marriage and family life. The
author defends this structure and seeks to find, in the wisdom
of tradition, some remedies for the ill which threaten it.

$6.95, paper

An Interesting Thought

The publication you have just finished reading is part of the apostolic efforts of the Society of St. Paul of the American Province. A small, unique group of priests and brothers, the members of the Society of St. Paul propose to bring the message of Christ to men through the communications media while living the religious life.

If you know a young man who might be interested in learning more about our life and mission, ask him to contact the Vocation Office in care of the Society of St. Paul, Alba House Community, Canfield, Ohio 44406 (phone 216/533-5503). Full information will be sent without cost or obligation. You may be instrumental in helping a young man to find his vocation in life.
An interesting thought.